DUCKS
across the
MOON

LIFE ON EIGHTY ACRES IN THE FLINT HILLS

Ken Ohm

DUCKS
across the
MOON

LIFE ON EIGHTY ACRES IN THE FLINT HILLS

by Dr. Ken Ohm

Front and back cover photos by:
  Brenda Culbertson — stargazr@holtonks.net

Sketches on pages:
  — 38, 62, 74, 79, 82, 91, 99, 119, 141, 222
  by Lars Szatko — chaosmonger@giantcomm.net

All other images where provided by the author.

ISBN 978-1-58597-473-3
Library of Congress Control Number: 2008927626

LEATHERS
PUBLISHING

4500 College Boulevard
Overland Park, Kansas 66211
888-888-7696
www.leatherspublishing.com

To my parents—

Frank and Leona,

who worked hard all their lives to give
my sister and me everything.

They were successful.

ACKNOWLEDGMENTS

This book would not have been possible without the support and encouragement of a number of people.

My dear wife, Ruth, not only provided me with emotional support, but read each page of the manuscript and offered ideas and suggestions that were invaluable. Further, her patience in sharing our computer at critical times allowed me to complete sections while the ideas were fresh and flowing. This sacrifice was no small gift as her priorities were at least as important as mine.

I want to express as well my gratitude to my editor, Don Pady. His editing expertise for my first book, "*Spatzies and Brass BBs: Life in a One-Room Country School*," continued in this book. Our weekly lunch sessions have been a delight—not only for improving the project but for reminding me of my purpose in bringing this book to completion. His unwavering enthusiasm carried me through times of doubt and uncertainty. He continues to be a valued friend.

My sister, Bonnie, and my friend, Adrienne Halpin, read and generously recommended changes and additions to the complete manuscript. They offered fresh ideas and helped shape and focus an improved narrative. Further, their moral support and encouragement was invaluable.

A number of my good friends, including Lyle Baker, Lee Anne Coester, Dick Driver, Ralph Jones, Frances Knowles and John Whittington and my son, Gary Ohm, read the manuscript and provided me with editorial suggestions, lost recollections, and corrections. Thanks to all of them for donating their time and expertise.

None of this could have been done without the full support of my publishers at Leathers Publishing, Madlyn Davis and Michele Rook. Their professionalism, constructive comments, and support deserve very special credit.

PREFACE

This book is a collection of very real stories that mirror the experiences of tens of thousands of American parents and children during the 1930s and 1940s in rural mid-America. Our world was the Kansas farm, the one-room school, the country church and the occasional trip to the little nearby town of Olpe or to the much larger and distant city of Emporia.

We were not hungry and we had clothes and shelter. Hard work made for sound sleep at night, and a reason to get up in the morning. Each member of the farm family had responsibilities or chores to be completed each day. Caring for animals and for crops gave us a feeling that we were needed and provided a sense of pride in the work we did.

Our immediate family—Dad, Mom, my sister Bonnie and me—was often temporarily expanded to include granddad, "Pop," and, on many different occasions, one or more of my eighteen aunts and uncles and twenty-nine cousins on my mother's side of the family. When illness or other interruptions occurred, families did not hesitate to ask for help in taking care of their family members until the crisis passed.

During the early years of my life, we lived on an oil lease in south-central Kansas, and then moved north to two different farms in the Flint Hills of Kansas. My most vivid memories were those from my mother's family farm. Dad was raised on a farm located only forty miles west, but all of his family moved away and rarely intersected our daily lives. On occasion, however, we visited some of Dad's relatives for a few days. Although these trips were rare, memories of lifestyles in distant cities made a lasting impression of another world with new things to be learned.

Reflecting on those days helps to focus on the deep love of parents for their children and the great sacrifices that parents in rural communities made for their children. Several of these chapters relate actual experiences of the author while others relay personal stories of parents, relatives and friends from their earlier lives. Some stories will be new to the world, and others retold, but all are written to be preserved as a part of America's rural history.

Dr. Ken Ohm
Summer, 2008
Ken.Ohm@Washburn.edu
Ken.Ohm@hotmail.com
Topeka, Kansas

TABLE OF CONTENTS

Part two — Learning from the Animals

Part three — The Outside World

Part four — Family Memories

Part One

Farm and Home

Life lessons, including triumph and defeat; health and illness; and interaction with neighbors, friends and relatives helped to guide my journey.

Miss Dalton — 1943

Chapter 1

A Cake Walk

"MISS DALTON, I can win a cake for you!" I shout. "That would be very nice, Kenny," she says with a laugh. "Here's a nickel. Win the next one for me."

When I was in first grade, my one-room school, Sunnyside, held evening fund-raising events three or four times each school year. On this particular occasion, a cake walk was featured and drew a large number of participants from the farms in the area.

Starting a full week before the gathering, the seven pupils in our school worked with our teacher, Miss Dalton, to prepare the school room. She was very excited during this time and gave us students a number of chores that we eagerly did. These duties included a thorough cleaning of the school room, but were to be done only after we completed all of our daily class assignments. These new activities actually inspired us to be more efficient and focused on our schoolwork. I am sure Miss Dalton was aware of that and worked our enthusiasm to achieve both goals.

Soot from the pot-bellied stove and dust blowing in from the windy prairie demanded considerable time and cleaning effort. Miss Dalton instructed each of us to bring a few rags from home to wash the desk tops, window sills and benches, as she, alone, scrubbed the floor with a mop and a pail of soapy water.

In addition to the cleaning chores, she also assigned the rather tedious job of numbering about twenty pages from a Big Chief writing tablet. Each student was given about three numerals to carefully draw—each filling one sheet of paper. We had no idea how they were to be used. Miss Dalton allowed the mystery to develop by suggesting that we would find out their use on the eventful evening.

Finally, Saturday arrived. My sister and I could not wait for the trip by car to the school that evening. After arriving, we ran into the schoolroom and observed a most unusual sight. The desks had been shoved to either side of the schoolroom, leaving a large open floor. At the other side of the room, about twenty beautifully decorated cakes formed a colorful row on a table. Fifteen numbered pages had been placed on the floor in a large circle. Since the only door into the school opened directly outside, the pages were kept from blowing away by a few small stones placed at the corners. Other kids soon arrived and together we walked carefully around the circle of numbers.

Most people were eager to contribute the nickel charge to play the game since this was an event to raise funds for the school. A wind-up Victrola record player was used to provide military marching music for the game. As the first round was about to begin, Dad gave Bonnie and me each a nickel. We gave the nickels to Miss Dalton and we each chose a numbered page to stand on. Within a few minutes, several others joined the circle. Miss Dalton held up one of the cakes and announced that it represented the prize for this first round. The music started to play and we slowly walked around the circle, stepping on one page and then the next. After about thirty seconds, Miss Dalton suddenly stopped the music. The players were instructed to stop walking and to look down to identify the numbered page they were standing on. Miss Dalton reached into a large pickle jar, drew out a number and called it out. I was astonished to hear the number of the page I was standing on!

I walked proudly to the side table and Miss Dalton handed the beautiful cake to me. Mom and Dad beamed as I handed it to them—and asked for another nickel. Dad gave me a slight frown, but reached in his pocket for another nickel and gave it to me. With building excitement, I again walked carefully around the circle, stopped with the music and listened for the winning number. My number was read for a second time. The crowd started to buzz as Dad gave me another nickel. The next game ended the same way, with me winning for the third straight time. By now, I had an enthusiastic following from the forty or more people in attendance, and I felt invincible. The term "in the zone," often used today, best described my feelings. I was absolutely certain that, when the music stopped, I would be standing on the winning number.

I approached Miss Dalton and volunteered to win her a cake. She happily agreed and put a nickel in the jar and started the music. A man from the crowd was selected to draw the number and read it out. I could not believe it. It was not my number. However, on that particular round, there were fewer players than numbers and no one was standing on the chosen number. He drew again, and it was mine. Another unforgettable moment! Miss Dalton handed me the cake and, bursting with pride, I handed it back to her. I received a few more nickels from other people during that evening, but never won again.

Later, when I became a student of mathematical probability, I figured that my chances of winning four games in a row was about one in twenty-thousand. Now, I look back over my seventy years and can remember only a few instances when I felt in such perfect "harmony with the universe." On rare occasions, when throwing the javelin, pitching a baseball game or taking a few college exams, I absolutely knew I would win the battle. However, most of the rest of my life has been "no cake walk!"

Chapter 2

"Pop" Schroeder

"GET THOSE HORSES in the barn right now!" Pop shouts. Cousin Lloyd and I wave our hands and try to shoo them in. Pop never has yelled at us before. Those horses better get in the barn right now or they won't get to eat tonight.

While much of my life has not been a "cake walk," my journey has been blessed with many people in my life, and has been guided by their influence. My maternal grandfather was one of them.

Nine children, twenty-eight grandchildren and fifty great-grandchildren called him Pop from their first memory. My kind and gentle grandfather had such an even temperament that when he occasionally lost his patience, it surprised people around him. When facing disappointment or grief, he seldom openly expressed his feelings. In early spring, when dandelions were in full, yellow bloom, he would protect them from being mowed or picked out. He declared, "they are beautiful and reflect God's wonderful art work."

Born on July 4th, 1875, in Mecklenburg, Schleswig-Holstein, Germany, he immigrated with his family to the Olpe, Kansas area in 1887. He did not begin to learn English until age seventeen while working both on his family's farm and hiring out as a laborer on other area farms.

Front row: Mother Leona, Aunt Clara and Aunt Gladys. Back row: Uncle Sam, Uncle Carl, Grandmother Regina and Grandfather John.

Pop married Regina Rathke on November 1ˢᵗ, 1899 and they had ten children. Their oldest son, Walter, was about twenty years older than their youngest child, Gladys. The demands of hard farm life required that each child help with work and chores, and they were assigned daily projects which were considered reasonable. Tragedy struck in 1927 when Regina, only fifty years old, began showing signs of heart failure. Walt and the oldest daughter, Nettie, carried a heavier load in the field and at home during that time as they helped care for the younger offspring. After several months of suffering, and with her children rallying around her to get farm work done, grandmother died in 1928. Soon, the older children married, left home and began their own families. The younger kids, including my mother—who was eleven at the time—then assumed critical duties to keep the farm and family going.

Pop insisted on regular school attendance for his children. Although he had no formal schooling, he knew that to improve the kids' lot in life, an education was necessary. So the kids walked each day to the one-room school nearly two miles away. One or two eventually attended high school in Emporia.

At one time or another, each of Pop's children lived with him after they had married and started families. While they struggled to establish financial independence, he offered them food and shelter, and they, in turn, worked on the farm and helped in the home.

When grandchildren arrived, he seemed delighted with their presence. He often asked the parents to "bring the little kids to see me." When they did, he lifted them on his lap and talked to them gently. My cousin, Geraldine, at about 9 years old, remembers seeing Pop with her knees and elbows scraped and scabbed over. Her embarrassment disappeared when Pop suggested "they will all be better before you get married." These kinds of reassurances were very important to all of us grandkids during those early years.

In his late seventies, Pop moved to town and into a little three-room house next to the railroad tracks on State Street. Although most of his children felt the noise from trains might disturb him, he said that he loved the sounds as they passed by. My mother did his washing each week until he died at the age of eighty-nine. During those days, she often found him in his rocking chair on the tiny front porch. He watched people as they walked past his house, and often called to them by name—especially children walking home from school. Pop even dressed in his Sunday pants and white shirt so he would be seen by others as a respectable man—one others would never have any reason to call just "an old man."

Chapter 3

Hot, Sticky Nights

WE ARE IN the barn trying to get the cows in for milking. It is so hot I can hardly breathe. "Dad, can we stay outside past bedtime tonight?" I plead. "It's going to be hot for several more days. We might as well get used to it," Dad replies. Well, at least he didn't say no. I can't wait to tell my sister that we might stay up late tonight.

During the hottest time of the late summer, with daily temperatures well over 100 degrees, my family often spent long days harvesting wheat, corn and hay. The wind caused dirt and stubble to blow across the fields. After a full day, the sharp pricks of the chaff and plant seeds penetrated our clothes and hurt the skin. Dousing the affected area with water sometimes provided temporary relief, but as the day progressed this remedy was short lived. We had no alternative but to keep at our work. We finally called it a day when either a finished job or darkness allowed us to stop.

When we came in from the fields, the late evening chores offered challenges that we hated to face. The evening temperatures often approached the highs for the day and, with no breeze at all, the thought of spending another hour or more in the confines of the milking barn depressed everyone. Although we often washed our hands and face before supper, when we headed back out to do chores, our clothes and bodies remained sweaty and dirty. With chores finally completed after an exhausting day, we slowly shuffled back to the house to face the late evening and nighttime heat.

No electricity meant no fans and no air-conditioning. The only relief during those hot July and August nights was to simply wait to go to bed in hopes that a cool breeze would pick up. We took baths once a week, whether summer or winter. On occasion, we would run down to the creek for a quick wade or swim. Otherwise we went to bed as we were—with grime and perspiration on our bodies. If a number of days passed since our last bath, our feet, ankles, neck and elbows were caked with dirt.

I remember lying on a thin blanket on the narrow concrete entrance outside our kitchen door. Although the air was a little cooler, mosquitoes and other insects attacked any bare spot of skin. They sometimes bit through our thin clothes or blankets. Heavy fatigue and insects finally ended the late-night adventure and drove us inside with faint hope of getting a comfortable night's sleep. Mom tried a number of times to show us how to use an old newspaper to fan ourselves. But, for us kids, it was more trouble than it was worth. Sometimes, especially when we had a visiting cousin or two, we tried talking to each other to distract from the heat, but Mom frowned on any visiting while in bed.

Once asleep, we often awakened to find our bodies sticking to the bed sheets. Moisture was trapped between our bodies and the sheets. When we tried to roll over or move, the sheets stuck to one side or the other, refusing to let go. The next morning broke well before our bodies were ready to get up. Mom and Dad arose an hour or so before the kids, and I often wonder how they could withstand the routine. Those long-ago hot nights are among the most painful memories of my childhood on the farm.

Chapter 4

Daily Prayers

"NOW I LAY me down to sleep. I pray the Lord my soul to keep. If I should die before I wake, I pray the Lord, my soul to take—Mom, I said my prayers!" "Good," she says. "I'll wake you up bright and early in the morning and we'll get ready for school".

Prayers before each meal and at bedtime were an absolute requirement. Generally, Mom or Dad had to hear them before they "counted." In the very early days of childhood, we said a brief German prayer that I never translated until adulthood. I imagine that my parents thought I knew what it meant, so there was no need to translate. From my point of view, I recall not really having any idea that it supposedly meant something—we just had to recite it each day. It was fun to say, *"Unser lieba Vater. Amen."* It means, "Our dear Father. Amen." It was simple enough to satisfy the short attention span of young children, but I believe it also gave my parents a feeling that they did their part to help save our souls in the event of some tragedy.

Evening prayers were said in bed with the lantern out—never at the side of the bed. We folded our hands under the blanket as we recited with our eyes closed. I do not remember Mom or Dad praying anywhere except in church and before meals. During this time, they were very solemn with no hint of pleasure or happiness showing on their faces. Even during great distress relating to failed crops, illnesses, deaths and funerals, I never heard a special call for divine intervention. It seemed truly, "his will be done." This was likely a reflection of their Lutheran upbringing and German heritage.

Once in school and able to recite longer prayers, we learned to say a common German prayer before every meal. It was, "*Come Lord Jesus, be our guest, and let this food to us be blessed. Amen.*" We said that prayer for years until a new pastor arrived at our Church, west of our nearby town of Olpe, Kansas. He suggested that we change the word, *food*, to *gifts*, so that it would be more inclusive and could be used on many other occasions in addition to meals. Only under rare circumstances did we hear another prayer in our home. On the occasion of a visit by an elder from our church, I recall the shock of hearing a prayer that he apparently made up as he talked. What a revelation to find other ways to talk directly to God!

One Christmas holiday, we made the long, one hundred mile trip by car to visit my uncle Con and his family in Winfield. This rare trip to see four older cousins was exciting, but also a little scary. While traveling in the car, Dad told my sister, Bonnie, and me that we must remain very quiet throughout the visit, and during meals we should never say a word unless we were asked a question. At the time for mealtime prayers, Dad told us to fold our hands on our laps—under the table, and bow our heads.

As we sat down for the first evening meal, uncle Con looked at the ten people around the table while he waited for complete silence. In a low voice he started, "Komm Herr Jesus, sei unsere Gast und segnet was Du uns bescheret hast. Amen." Although Mom and Dad occasionally spoke to each other in German, my sister and I had never heard such a prayer at the dinner table. We heard this prayer several more times during the following two days. Although nearly the same prayer we had been saying in English for a few years, the rhythm or melody of the German syntax was irresistible to my sister and me as we tried to duplicate it. On the way back to the farm, we were a little too loud as we sang in the back seat of the car, "Come Harry Hayzoos, sigh and circus..." I do not remember my dad ever being more upset with us. He made it very clear that our translations were a direct affront to God, and that we should feel very sorry to have "used His name in vain."

As was generally the case, I never understood the mysterious workings of the Lord. However, my dad's outburst to our song made an impression that has lasted a lifetime. It became clear to me that communicating with God was most serious. If I expected to have His help, I must respect and honor Him. From my early adult years to the present time, I have found prayer very comforting during difficult and trying times.

Chapter 5

AS I WALK in from chores, the phone rings—three shorts and two longs. It's our number! Mom answers, "Oh, no, not again." She quickly hands the phone to Pop. "We'll be right over," he shouts. He hangs up the receiver and tells us that the cattle are in the Jones' pasture again.

Our barbed-wire fence always seemed on the verge of breaking. The saying "the grass is always greener on the other side of the fence" seemed to describe the opinion of our cattle. To make matters worse, when one of the cows found a way through the fence, most of the herd followed. Our first duty was to find the herd, round them all up and, hopefully, drive them back through the same opening. It was generally the responsibility of the owner of the escaped cattle to quickly fix the fence between the neighbors. A temporary patch over the hole would be constructed.

Once the need for a fencing project was determined, days of preparation were required before the actual work could start. Large rolls of fencing wire and one-inch staples had to be purchased from the hardware store in Olpe and new posts selected and cut from nearby hedge-rows.

Without mechanical help fence repairs required at least two workers to do the job. Mom frequently volunteered to help when Dad and Pop had other farm projects. On one occasion, Mom, Bonnie, and I worked on a small fencing project in the pasture. All at once, Mom let out a yell, spotting a rattlesnake just a few feet away. She threw her hammer at it, but the hammer missed. The snake encircled it, hissed, and refused to move.

We were all frightened and ran back to the house waiting until the next day to go back. By that time, the snake had left, so we retrieved the hammer and the job was finally completed. To this day, over sixty years later, the frightful vision of that large rattlesnake coiled around the hammer seems as clear as yesterday.

My family did all fence repairs on our farm, but some of our neighbors could afford to hire extra help. One pair of bachelor brothers, the Sagers, was famous throughout the four or five county area as the very best fence builders, and they were the top choice when help was needed. If Dad had heroes other than Max Schmeling, Joe Lewis and Babe Ruth—they were the Sagers. We spent many evening meals hearing stories of creative fencing techniques supposedly invented by the Sager brothers. As a kid, I found these discussions very interesting. Mom and Bonnie also seemed to enjoy the tales, and they would smile and nod their heads.

I tried to imagine the two men working on the pasturelands day after day. Whether it was a severely hot July afternoon or in a near-blizzard in winter, the "Sager Boys" worked in all seasons. And, whether they were fencing the crest of a hill or over a stream or creek, the brothers' ingenuity was revered. They had even built special rope and pulley systems to stretch the wire tightly between the fence posts.

When we were traveling the Flint Hills, the Sagers' fences were instantly recognizable by the sharp, straight lines of the barbed wires. If we were especially fortunate, we might spot them working in the pasture. Once or twice my dad and I stopped to visit with them for a few minutes. "How you doing?" Dad asked. The brothers would both rise stiffly from their working position, offer a handshake, and answer, "Just fine." Even on a very hot summer day, they would wear flannel shirts with long sleeves, straw hats pulled down just above their eyes and cowboy boots. Both in their eighties, they were slim in build and their skin was heavily tanned and wrinkled. Their personalities showed a certain peace and contentment that I recall to this day. Perhaps spending a lifetime working outdoors in the Flint Hills gave them a sense of oneness with nature for which most of us spend a lifetime searching.

I felt similar "peak experiences" while working alone in the countryside of a ranch during my early high school days—the quietness in the vast land, the brilliant blue sky that went on forever, the occasional call of a bird or lowing of a cow in the distance, the feeling of smallness in an unending universe, yet at one with the vast unknown. The rare view of an airplane far overhead was the only reminder that other humans were present on the planet—Zen and the Art of Fencing.

A Sagars' invention.

Chapter 6

Slingshots and Inner Tubes

WE ARE DRIVING to Emporia today. This will be exciting watching the people walk along the sidewalks. "Oh, no," Dad shouts, "We have a flat tire." It will be a long time now before we get to Emporia. Dad quickly fixes the tire.

On that particular day, Dad had just completed the tire repair, and we had driven only a few more miles when another tire went flat! Dad's anger usually involved a barely audible mumble. This time though, he erupted with a shout to the heavens. He pulled the car to the side of the road and the four of us once again stepped out. Bonnie and I knew enough to clear the site and walk several yards in a ditch along a nearby field. Mom stayed by the car to provide sympathy and understanding to Dad's plight.

Dad slid the car jack under the car to lift the back tire off the ground. He then used a large wrench to remove the lug nuts and free the wheel. With what seemed like great strength, Dad inserted a thin, iron bar to separate the rim of the wheel from the tire. Reaching into the tire, he pulled out the limp, rubber inner tube. He quickly found that the hole was small enough to patch. Of course, that was good news because we would soon be on our way to town. Bonnie and

Road repair.

I were a little disappointed, however, because we were sometimes given badly-damaged inner tubes to play with.

We found many uses for a discarded inner tube, but the most popular was to make large, thick rubber bands for play guns and slingshots. We borrowed a pair of scissors from Mom's sewing basket and cut one-inch strips around the tube's diameter. After cutting as many as a dozen rubber rings, blisters often formed on our fingers from the scissors' handle.

Dad cut one-by-six inch boards into shapes of either small rifles or long-barrel pistols. The key was to have a groove cut into the end of the gun's barrel to hold one end of the inner tube band. The other end of the band stretched tightly to the back of the barrel and onto a sloping wood projection. Then, with the weapon properly "loaded," a flip of the shooter's thumb freed the rubber band as it "shot" toward the target.

Depending on how close a cousin might be while running by, a direct hit could produce a sting and a red mark on the skin. Rubber band guns were not considered nearly as dangerous, however, as a slingshot.

Constructed of an inner tube rubber band and a well-selected Y-shaped tree limb, a lethal weapon can be produced. The basic design was handed down from older to younger cousins, but no two slingshots were alike. Whatever the specific design and size, a major problem concerned the attachment of the two loose ends of a band to the upper tips of the "Y." We often wedged the band snugly into cut grooves in the tips of the slingshot. When string or baling wire was available, we wrapped the tips tightly to secure the bands.

If, while cutting the bands from an inner tube, we planned to build a slingshot, we carefully cut the band wider at a central location to hold the projectiles. The problem with this rubber "pouch" was that the "ammo" often stuck as it left on its flight to the target. To offset this problem, we tied pieces of leather from old belts or shoes to the rubber bands. If the leather's pouch attachment was successful, it made the slingshot more accurate.

Most often we chose smooth, rounded rocks for our ammunition. They seldom traveled far because of their irregular shapes and surfaces. We attempted to shoot various animals and birds with little success. But we had great fun setting up tin cans on fence posts for targets and having contests to determine the best shooter.

On occasion, one of the cousins might find a steel ball bearing on the dirt floor of the shop or in the yard. We immediately recognized these as "exceptional" slingshot projectiles. Indeed, they traveled so far that we had difficulty finding and reusing them. Although rock ammunition did not seem to cause alarm, if one of the kids mentioned finding a ball bearing to a parent, we were all lectured on its danger and warned that "we might put out an eye." Fortunately, we never had a serious injury, although we heard stories of others not so lucky who were seriously injured by these homemade weapons.

Chapter 7

BONNIE AND I jump into the back seat of our 1935 Chevy. Right between us is the smooth, white block of salt we just bought from Brinkman's Hardware store in Olpe. As we start down Main Street, we both lean over and take a lick on the block. Mom yells back at us, "You better not do that. You are going to get sick!"

In each of our pastures, we regularly supplied a 40-pound block of salt for the cattle. Dad would either build a wooden box or platform to support the block, or—if he found just the right-cut cooking-stove log—he used that instead.

The adult cattle required regular access to salt and would do just about anything to get it. With long, hot summer days grazing in the pasture, salt was vital to their survival. If we occasionally did not notice a salt block had been used up, the cattle pawed the ground and actually licked the dirt that contained salt particles. They butted their heads and tried to push other cattle away from the site. Their efforts disturbed us when white slobber dripped from their mouths. When unsuccessful in finding salt, they made every effort to break through the fencing into a neighboring pasture. We occasionally found an animal with severe cuts on its body from the barbs on the fencing as it tore its way through the fence. Most of the time the animal was left untreated, but if severe injuries threatened its life, it was herded into the barnyard for treatment.

Under normal circumstances, the ground around the salt block became well worn from the cattle spending time sharing the block. Well-formed paths from all parts of the pasture led to the salt lick. A rather deep depression often formed around the block when mud caused by rains was tracked out of the area on the cattle hooves to the adjoining pasture.

When we drove the milking cows into the barn each day, we had occasion to walk past the salt block. The cupping on the block, formed by the cow tongues, was quite unique and it appeared as if a fine-tuned machine had smoothed out a four or five-inch diameter hollow. We ran our fingers along the inside of the cup to feel the curious design. If it had rained the previous night, and if it were very early, the cupping created by the cow tongues filled with water. Then, the first cow to slurp it up realized that salt water was a real treat. We noticed, however, that little calves did not use the salt lick because they received their supply of salt from their mother's milk.

Salt lick areas can be spotted from the air, especially in the winter when the salt helps melt surrounding snow. Long after I left the farm, heavy chains were placed between two posts to support bags of insecticides, placing them near the salt licks so that the cattle could rub against the bags. In later years, as I practiced for emergency landings in my airplane, I approached the upside of a hill to within a few feet above the ground. But when I crested the hill, I saw straight ahead of me a long chain wrapped with canvas. I pulled up just in time and cleared it by inches. I have often thought how unfortunate it would have been to have a salt lick as my final resting place.

Chapter 8

Water Witcher

"RUN IN AND get a little mirror from Mom; I want to show you something," Dad orders. I enter the kitchen and see Mom standing near the stove. "Dad says I need a mirror to help him at the well," I shout. Mom reaches to a shelf and hands me a hand mirror, warning me to be careful not to break it. Running quickly back to the well, I hand the mirror to Dad. He asks me to look down into the well. I rise on my tiptoes and lean over the wooden side of the well. Just then, Dad reflects the sun's image onto the water surface, deep below. I see such a bright light that I am frightened and my legs feel shaky. Dad starts to tell me a story of how he dug a water well.

As a young man in the 1920s, Dad teamed with neighbors to hand dig a water well on his father's farm. Fresh drinking water had been found only twenty feet deep on nearby farms. His family hoped they would be equally successful. But, with no mechanical digging devices, picks and shovels and many days of backbreaking work were required.

The first step in well digging was to determine a suitable site. It had to be within walking distance of the house and, of course, provide an adequate water supply. Since it was not a simple matter to find

This is the spot.

water within an easy-digging depth, considerable effort was made to choose a highly-probable location.

Although most Kansas farmers were deeply religious and fearful of magic or witchcraft, many still hired a water-witcher to help determine the best well-site. Witchers' success rates in this part of the Flint Hills were high enough to merit their employment. Dad said that a witcher from distant Marion County was hired by most of the local farmers because his water-finding reputation was so good. He charged two dollars to pinpoint a site—but offered no guarantee that water would be found. Dad's father contacted him and hired him to find the digging site. Plans were made for his travel to our farm.

Word spread to the neighbors several days before the witcher's arrival. Some traveled many miles to view the action. The excitement rivaled that of visits by doctors, ministers and politicians. The neighbors seemed to revere the ability of the witcher and stood quietly by at the scene.

As part of his preparation, the witcher carefully quizzed Dad's father as to where he might want the well dug. He then retrieved a Y-shaped willow branch—some three feet long—from his truck. Grabbing either side of the top of the "Y" with his hands, he pointed the single branch forward. He took on a serious and focused look as he slowly walked along the proposed site. On occasion, the branch would suddenly shake and bend gently to the ground. The witcher temporarily stopped and then continued walking. He then returned across the field. After he crisscrossed the site several times, those watching started whispering that the exact spot would become evident when the willow branch dived downward each time the witcher passed by it. It was rare when the spot was more than a few yards from the owner's preference.

As if coming out of a trance, the witcher finally stopped at the proposed location and, breathing a heavy sigh, stated that "a good well will be found directly below this spot!" With smiles all around, the crowd gasped and broke into applause. A small stake was driven into the ground at the exact spot and, as part of his mystic aura, the witcher left quickly. He simply accepted his two dollars and drove away.

With the excitement at such a pitch, a circle some 8 ft in diameter was scratched into the dirt around the stake, and a number of spectators immediately started to dig. Most of the farmers eventually had to return to their own chores, but a few stayed on to help for several more hours, finally finding an excellent water source which was used for almost fifty years.

Many years later, while developing a housing project in Wyoming, I found it necessary to drill a water well to supply some fifteen homes. I recalled those stories of my father and decided to hire a locally famous water-witcher. I invited friends to the site on that early summer afternoon, and we watched the witcher follow almost the same routine as Dad had earlier described.

The witcher concluded that a major water source could be found below either of two locations on the land site—one of which was already my top priority. He added that it would take a very deep well to find water but it would be worth it. I handed him his twenty-five dollar fee and decided to hire a professional well-digging company.

After several days of digging to a few hundred feet down, a spectacular artesian well was found and continued to supply the development for more than twenty years. Thanks, Dad!

Chapter 9

The Water Well Fridge

"KENNY, GO GET me the butter in the well bucket, and be very careful," Mom commands. I quickly run out the kitchen door and to the well. I start pulling on the heavy rope, slowly lifting the bucket from the water below. After several short pulls, I see the bucket nearing the top and, grabbing it with its wire handle, lift it to the side of the well. Inside are eggs, a few jars of milk, some lunchmeat and a jar of butter. I take out the butter and slowly lower the bucket back until it touches the water and gently floats.

The well was covered with one-inch by twelve-inch boards, about six feet long. This was to protect the water below from dust and other debris. When fetching the bucket from below, it was necessary to remove one of the boards. With seasonal changes the ground water flushed out old water in the well, replacing it with safe drinking water. Finally, feed-lots in the area, changing ground-water level, and contamination—such as varmints falling to the bottom of the well—made the water undrinkable.

By the time we moved to mother's home farm in the early 1940s, the cold water in the well was used only for providing an excellent storage for dairy products and meats and to supply our chickens with drinking water. Dad helped me practice the trick of "sinking the bucket." Just as the two-gallon bucket touched the surface, the rope was given a little "jerk" in order to tilt the bucket to make it sink and fill. Over a period of several days and lots of frustration, I was able to gather a full pail of water and lift it to the top.

To provide a safe, cooling environment for foods, we lowered the bucket until it rested several inches in the water. This arrangement protected the food for several days at a time. As a kid, I was honored to lift or lower the bucket. Because a slip of the rope might result in the loss of a very important food supply, we took this responsibility very seriously.

In later years, I shared my childhood memories of our old water well with my ninety-year old mother. I described my fear of the darkness and the dank smell of the water below. I told her of my fleeting glances at the stone lining of the well and how I shuddered as my eyes followed the rough ridges down to the water's surface. Mom paused for a moment and, with a very serious expression on her face, began a terrifying story that she had never before shared.

When she was about fifteen years old, she felt a desperate need for adventure. As is typical of so many teenagers of today, the search for independence and individual expression was very strong—even seventy-five years ago. While retrieving a bucket of water from the well, she had an uncontrollable urge to climb down along the wall to the water, some twenty feet below. Her first move was to sit with feet dangling over the wall's edge. She then placed one foot on a protruding rock and, holding on to the well's wooden rim, dropped her other foot to a rock a few feet lower. She continued downward for a number of steps, finding secure handholds on the rocks. At some point, she found her legs becoming more and more spread with each downward step and panic nearly overtook her. She carefully returned step by step to the top of the well and lifted herself over the side. She was emotionally exhausted by the experience and felt she had escaped death by the narrowest of margins.

Finishing her story, she was quiet for a moment and then said, "Stupid, stupid, stupid!"

Restless at fifteen.

Team Work

Chapter 10

Making Hay

"IF YOU ARE going with me this morning, you will have to find a long sleeved shirt and some gloves," Dad said. This is really going to be fun. I will get to watch and to help build a great big haystack. Some of my cousins will be there too. I hope Dad lets me walk on top of the haystack.

Starting in late July and running through August, cutting and "putting up" hay was a dusty, sticky and deathly hot job. Snakes, turtles, birds, rabbits, bees, and an occasional coyote interfered with the workers on almost every haying day.

We had two hayfields—one contained about 30 acres of prairie hay directly to the north of our farmhouse and the other contained a 30 acre alfalfa plot across the gravel road to the southwest. The first step in harvesting hay was to determine the right day to cut it down. "Making hay while the sun shines" truly foretold the work of the day. Weather played a key role in the choice of the hay day because 30 or more acres of freshly-cut hay on the ground with an incoming rain, or even a heavy dew, could be disastrous. If wet hay lays on the ground for more than a day or two, it becomes moldy, foul-smelling and unusable. Prairie hay remains quite sturdy and requires only minimal care, but alfalfa is very sensitive to heat and humidity. On a hot day, alfalfa is dry enough for harvesting for only a short time, but not so dry that the valuable leaves crumble and are lost. We chose the two fastest and friskiest horses for this critical and timely job of mowing alfalfa.

The mower cut a six-foot swath back and forth over the length of the field. When reaching the end of a row, the team of horses was turned by slowing the horse in the direction of the turn or by speeding up the other. The mower consisted of a long arm with sharp blades oscillating back and forth, snipping the hay stems a few inches above the ground. We sometimes cut through a nest in an old clump of hay where rabbits or birds lived. Coyotes generally ran several yards ahead of us as we approached. The mower often struck animals and either killed or maimed them. Kids would be disturbed, but most of the adult drivers just kept cutting hay. When my cousins and I observed an injured animal, Dad stopped the mower and carefully carried it to a safer location.

After the proper drying time, a horse or tractor-driven hay rake gathered the hay into long windrows. Our horse-drawn rake was called a "dump-rake" and measured about twelve feet wide, holding a number of heavy, curved wire teeth. The operator rode on a metal seat directly above the teeth. The rake pulled the loose hay for a span of 10 or 20 feet and then, using a lever arm, dumped it. This process continued across the hayfield and, depending on how thick the hay was, might form as many as forty or fifty rows. The rake then turned around at the far side of the field and traveled back, again dumping hay at the same interval as its initial crossing. These fifty rows then formed long, relatively straight windrows ready for the next operation.

At about this time, neighbors Gramke, Rathke and Jones were alerted and asked to help finish the shared job. Most often they would come the next morning, after the raking was completed, to help build the haystacks. A forked "haybuck" drove its wooden teeth under the hay and pushed it from the windrows to the site previously selected for the stack. The hay was loaded directly onto an "overshot" hay stacker. With teeth much like the haybuck, the stacker lifted the hay onto the stack by means of rope and a team of horses. Some of the kids of age eight or so might take charge of this lifting chore, and actually direct the horses and the stacker.

Normally, three or four men with pitchforks walked the site and spread the hay around the perimeter of the twenty-foot circle, then gradually filled the area within. Each load was dumped onto the stack, so the height of the haystack gradually increased. I was allowed to walk on the level but rising surface of the stack until it reached about four feet. At that height, Dad lowered me to the ground and, carefully watching the equipment, found a safe location from which I watched without getting in the way.

We needed several hours to build the haystack high enough to "top out." This might be as high as 20 to 25 feet. A fall from that height could result in serious injury. The packing and careful sloping, at the top, required strict attention by the men. The design of the top of the stack should allow rain to run off as much as possible without destroying the hay in the upper stack. This always seemed to be a tense time for the workers. They spent an entire day working the stacks, so by the end of the day—the most critical part—fatigue and weariness had already set in from the heat and dust. Somehow, I remember that at the end of most haying days, the workers were not in a good mood.

On one particular day, I recall Dad was very disturbed about a missing pitchfork—and no one could remember where it went. It was finally concluded after much searching that it was covered up somewhere in the haystack and could not be recovered until the haystack was used for feed. Because of that experience, the well-worn saying, "finding a needle in a haystack," became one we all used during our lifetimes.

Chapter 11

Safety in a Manger

"MOM, WILLIE KEEPS snorting and stomping his feet whenever I walk by his pen," I whine. "He scares me every time I see him." Mom looks at me and says that I should not worry because our bull, Willie, can never get out and hurt me. I remember her telling me about her sister Clara and a mean bull. I could never do what Mom did!

With good weather and a positive response from neighbors, three or four haystacks might be constructed over a period of a few days, providing "one-age hay." Some winter seasons required using hay in all the stacks, while at other times, a full haystack or two might remain standing after the winter feeding season. We made every effort all during the year to use this hay to either feed sheltered animals held for butchering, or for bulls and horses which were separated for various reasons. Each of the sheltering sheds had steel corner posts, tin roofs, and wooden siding, and opened to the south for protection against prevailing winds.

We had a hay manger in each of our three separate pens. Rather than tossing hay on the ground as feed, hay was loaded into the open top of the mangers. This provided some protection from the weather and from feeding cattle that might tread on the hay. These 10 by 15 foot structures had four heavy logs, vertically buried with one end a few feet into the ground, acting as corners. Along each side and along the ends, several 2 by 6 inch boards were nailed in place horizontally. The mangers had a gap between the boards of about one foot that allowed cattle to reach through and feed on the hay.

One of the oft-repeated stories of my mother's childhood involved one of her older sisters, Clara, who strayed into a bullpen. When Mom heard her sister screaming, she ran to the pen to find that her sister had crawled into the manger to get away from the bull. With the bull snorting and sprinting up and down on opposite sides of the manger, Mom decided to take action. Screaming loudly and waving her hands, she entered the pen and charged toward the bull. Her sister was then able to run to the fence and climb over it while the bull was distracted. Mom ran directly past the bull and climbed over the fence on the far side of the pen—just as the bull charged toward her. For the rest of her life, Clara gave Mom credit for saving her life on that frightening day over eighty years ago.

Chasing Leona.

Chapter 12

WE ARE HIDING in the haymow, looking down through a crack in the wall. "Shush, do not say a word. They might hear us," Lloyd said. Don, Edgar and Darrell are walking under us. Boy, would they be surprised if they knew we were watching them!

The broad, empty floor of the haymow was a tempting play area in early spring. To reach the mow, we had to climb a seven-step, vertical ladder—constructed from boards and nailed to the wall studs of the barn. After some sixty years of sliding baled and loose hay across the worn one-by-four inch boards, the light shining through the door and cracks in the walls created a sparkle on the smooth floor. At times, the floor looked almost like glass and I remember trying to skate across it in my shoes as I might do on a frozen creek.

The boards used for the barn's siding were nailed in place with no overlap, so over the years cracks developed which let in light and wind. Even on very cold days, however, the mow provided protection from the elements when Mom or another adult ordered us to "get out of the house." The beautiful view from this second floor, especially to the south, contained the large open area below the rise of the farm site. Homemade bows and arrows had increased range and snowballs could be pitched to much greater distances with this added elevation.

Directly under the mow were stalls for the milk-cows and horses. Knot holes and cracks in the floor provided opportunity to drop grain, sticks, and other objects onto the animals' heads and, especially, their ears. What great fun to see one of the horses wiggle its ears at first impact, and then finally throw its head back and forth while we continued to drop objects on it.

One late summer day, several cousins and I played in the mow. I decided to jump out the door onto a large stack of loose hay just below. Before anyone could warn me, I jumped successfully and was congratulating myself when my cousins above me screamed. They shouted that I had missed a pitch fork by just a matter of inches! Looking to one side, I saw the gleaming four prongs of a large fork. It had apparently been thrown down, handle first, by someone who did not expect anyone to jump on it. For some reason, the cousins would not forget the incident and reported it to my parents and several other adults. They came running out of the house to check the situation. To this day, many of those who stood around the haystack remember the time when I made a serious error in judgment—and narrowly missed a very serious accident.

In recent years, the barn and the haymow have been used as a background for photographs of graduating seniors, weddings and anniversaries. Some photos, taken from ground level, show especially interesting images of the subject rustically framed by the haymow door. Boards, worn smooth from hay bales and from animals rubbing against them, surround doorways and stall openings. Now, they are being eyed for use in specialty dens and other rustic rooms in area homes.

Even as the barn continues to deteriorate, pitchforks, hay hooks, branding irons and other antique tools still hang from its walls. When the barn finally collapses, which it almost certainly will, the last remnants of the physical structure will be gone, but the vivid memories will live on.

Chapter 13

I TRIED TO run the whole way. School seemed to last forever today. But now I get to help shock the wheat. As I cross the bridge over Shaw Creek, I see a tractor at the far end of the field. Maybe Dad will let me pick up the shocks and stack them.

We had waited for this day for a numbers of weeks. Finally, Dad determined that the sea of grain was ready to harvest. The binder arrived at day break, pulled by the Stuttle's green, John Deere tractor. On my walk to school that day, I could hear the put-put of the tractor engine. Even at the full one-mile distance, a distinctive sound could be heard in my little one-room school. The other kids and I talked excitedly about the fun we would have in the wheat field.

When I arrived at the wheat field, I ran close to the binder. Dad greeted me with a wave, and stopped the tractor. He jumped down and explained how the binder worked.

Dad showed me the roll of binder twine, with its distinctive smell, that had been placed over a vertical metal rod. One loose end was threaded through a tiny hole and into the tying mechanism. He pointed to the freshly-oiled front-end cutting sickle which led into standing grain. He demonstrated how the strands of wheat fell onto a revolving canvas belt carrying them into the machine's entry tunnel.

After calling out to me to move some distance away, he started up the tractor and pulled the binder into a heavy stand of wheat. As the machine captured the cut stocks, and after lots of bouncing and groaning inside the machine, two or three bundles at a time dropped along the ground. Dad shouted that I could join two of the workers who walked beside a long row of tied wheat bundles. I easily learned how to pick up two bundles, one in each hand. I entwined the wheat heads and pointed them upward, and made the two bundles stand on end. Adding six bundles to the standing two, created a tee-pee shaped stack. Lastly, a final cap bundle was placed at the top to provide protection from the rainy weather. We produced a sight across that 40-acre site that reminded me of pictures of Indian villages. New combines were introduced in the following year. This was our last wheat shocking experience, although we continued to shock corn for many more years.

As darkness fell, Dad invited me to ride on the tractor as it pulled the binder to the shelter of nearby trees. We walked the one-half mile together up the gentle hill to our house. We said very little, but I could tell that Dad was proud of my efforts that afternoon. I had a feeling of great accomplishment.

Binding Wheat

Chapter 14

The Threshing Crew

I KNOW MY flannel shirt is in this drawer somewhere. The thresh-ing crew will arrive soon and I want to be outside so I can see them bring in the big machine. It's going to be a hot day, but Mom says this winter shirt will keep me from itching. I run out of the house and I see the strange looking machine pulled behind the neighbor's tractor. It crosses directly in front of our house and stops right next to the silo. This is going to be a fun day!

Ah, Saturday! I did not have to go to school. Soon I would have my first experience watching wheat and oats separated from straw. The threshing machine arrived at daybreak, so we finished chores and had breakfast very early. The threshing machine produced great amounts of dust, so every effort was made to orient it so the workers stood upwind from the action. Most farmers of the time developed considerable skill at predicting daily weather, and Dad used his to determine the exact position of the machine. On this occasion, he quickly concluded that the wind would be from the southwest and the best location would be just west of the silo. The dust would then blow toward the feedlot near our barn and then across the pasture.

Several men and women from nearby farms and hired hands from the area gathered at our farm as the monster machine arrived and rumbled up the long lane from the county road to our house. It was my first close-up look at a thresher. The iron wheels and metal body was the biggest I had ever seen.

Mom and the other women started very early that day to prepare a large noontime dinner for the crew. One of the hired hands brought two, 100-pound blocks of ice from the grocery store in Olpe, where he lived. Five-pound chunks were broken off the block to add to a 10-gallon crock filled with sliced lemons, sugar and water—making a welcomed lemonade drink. Most of the crew either had their own tin cup or a glass to be filled with a common dipper from the crock.

It took the entire morning for the ladies to assemble the noon-day meal for more than fifteen people. Mom's oldest sister, Nettie, arrived early to prepare dozens of her special homemade buns. Thick slices of ham were placed within the buns to make a hearty sandwich lunch treat. A clean bed sheet spread over the edge of a hayrack acted as a serving table. Someone purchased several watermelons in Olpe a few days before the threshing began and these were placed in a nearby stock tank, along with the rest of the ice, to cool. Cold watermelon provided delightful dessert before the long afternoon continued with only occasional stops for cold lemonade or water. To this day, I often hear and use the expression, "enough to feed a threshing crew," to describe a Thanksgiving or Christmas dinner spread!

Bundles of oats or wheat had been previously stacked neatly in shocks in the nearby fields. The hundreds of these bundles were the target of several horse-drawn wagons. Generally, two men would throw the bundles onto the rack wagon. The horses pulling the wagon followed the rows naturally and did not need a driver. Lifting a bundle in each hand, the men tossed them onto the rack while walking along-side. A full rack wagon, carrying a few hundred bundles, was then driven to the threshing site. Since the machine's intake belt was some ten feet off the ground, the rack wagon came alongside at a proper height for the two men to toss the bundles into the large mouth.

The threshing machine shook and roared with each bundle. A steady stream of wheat or oats poured from the canvas spout at the side. The grain was captured in gunny sacks one by one on another rack wagon. This very intense job of placing an empty sack under the spout and then quickly sliding it away, then replacing it with another empty sack — required at least two men. The filled sacks were neatly stacked on the wagon floor. When a wagon was filled, it was driven to the granary where the sacks were emptied, before returning for another load. As the straw streamed out the back of the machine, two men with pitchforks worked steadily to throw the straw onto an open wagon. The full wagon was pulled by two horses to the nearby feedlot where the straw was spread over the ground.

The threshing job took several days to complete, and the end of each day was very special. After the day's work, most of the threshers ran down to the creek a few hundred yards away and jumped in with their clothes on in an effort to get rid of as much of the itchy chaff as possible. They would then strip and jump in again, hand-picking some of the burrs from their clothes before putting them back on. If we were threshing oats, itching from the chaff felt miserable. Wheat was not nearly as troublesome, but still required major cleaning each evening.

Most of the workers traveled home for the night, although several — especially the younger ones — stayed overnight and slept on the rack wagons. I recall very little activity in the late evening; they were exhausted after the long day's work. The ladies returned each day to start the cooking process all over again with very little change in menu. Ham was most favored because it could be exposed to the outdoor air for long periods without becoming tainted.

When I lived on the farm, store-bought flour was affordable, so harvested grain was either sold or used to feed our own cattle. Just a few years earlier, however, some of the wheat was saved to make flour. A gunny sack full of wheat was poured into a three-foot square screen box. The box was placed on a stand a few feet above the ground and shaken back and forth by hand. The screen allowed the grain to pass through, but captured most of the left-over chaff. This screening process was repeated many times before the wheat was considered clean enough to be ground into flour. The grinding was done at a mill in town some twenty miles away.

The threshing day experience is one that has stayed with me over the years. I can still feel the excitement of so many people working and eating together and then seeing the results in mounds of golden grain. Days after the work was completed, we kids occasionally walked barefooted up to our knees in the cool, soft piles of grain. Even wading in cool spring water did not have the same, exciting effect as the feeling of the tiny grains squeezing between our toes!

Chapter 15

Filling Silo

IT IS WARM under my covers, but I will have to get up soon to go to school. I hear some noise outside. I remember now: It is Saturday. I get to help fill the silo today!

September on the farm was an exciting time: we brought the last crop of hay into the barn or put it in a haystack, took several days to thresh the wheat and oats, and finally filled the silo to complete the harvest.

In the fall, the first priority for farmers was to make sure that a sufficient supply of feed would be available for their livestock during the winter months. Before any corn was harvested for its grain, the silo had to be filled.

For several weeks before scheduling a three-day period to fill our 120-ton silo, corn fields were carefully checked to determine when the crop was ready to be chopped and made into silage—a kind of pickled corn. Farmers checked the kernels with their thumbnail. If a "doughy" core of a kernel was found, they knew it was time for the silo harvest. If muddy fields, or something else caused a delay in harvesting, the kernels often became too hard to make good silage. We countered this, on occasion, by driving our corn wagons by our water tank and throwing buckets of water over the dried corn.

Ready for the silo.

In the early morning of the first day, a chopper, blower and two horse drawn wagons were brought in by neighbors—all in exchange for labor and machinery for their own harvesting project. Only one or two distant neighbors owned all the necessary equipment to fill their silo. They only had to hire a few extra laborers and did not need to share their effort with other farmers.

Mom and the helpers' wives organized the large noontime meals for the silo crew as they had done a few weeks earlier for the threshing crew.

The actual silo filling generally took about three or four days. The first day was devoted to connecting the chopper to the blower and preparing cutters, wagons, horses and tractors to bring the corn in from the field. Freshly-cut corn provided the best silage. A corn binder cut and tied about twelve to fifteen corn stalks into each bundle. The binder dropped off four or five bundles at a time along the corn rows. One or two laborers picked up the bundles and tossed them toward the back of a slowly moving, horse drawn, rack wagon.

After filling the wagon, the loaders hopped on the wagon and drove the horses to the silo site. The chopper was powered by a tractor which was cranked and started by hand. The bundles were tossed in one at a time, directly off the bundle wagons. Each corn stalk, including the corn and cobs, was chopped into small, square-inch pieces. These were funneled into the blower which then elevated the silage to the top and over the side into the silo. After a few minutes, a worker climbed through the lowest of about ten, vertical windows on one side of the silo. He spread and packed the silage as it slowly filled the silo. Once the level reached the base of the window, he placed a window cover over the opening.

The 18 by 24 inch, double-panel window covering was constructed of 1-by-4 inch boards. The worker carried a small milk bucket half-filled with thick mud to provide a tight seal around the opening. This kept oxygen from damaging the fermenting silage after the fill, and it worked very well. In fact, when retrieving the silage, no differences could be detected, whether the silage came from next to the window covering or next to the concrete blocks of the silo's wall. This step-by-step process of filling the silo continued throughout the day.

After each wagon emptied its load, it would return to the corn field to pick up another load. With the equipment so difficult to start up, the chopper and blower engines were just throttled down and not turned off while waiting for the next wagon to arrive.

Finally, after about twelve hours, with the sun setting and chores to be done, the workers returned to their homes. Plans were often made to either meet again the next day to continue the current job, or to start the process over again at the farm of one of the workers.

The two weeks following the silo fill was a time when children were forbidden to walk near the silo. We knew that dangerous gasses likely escaped from the fermenting silage which, in some instances, had killed unsuspecting farmers! Years after I left the farm, scientists determined that nitrogen dioxide was the primary toxic gas formed in open-top silos like ours. Although death can occur immediately, farmers might not suffer symptoms similar to pneumonia until two to six weeks after exposure. I often wonder how many farm deaths were attributed to pneumonia from other causes when they were actually caused by silo gasses.

A sad story was told to us almost every silo-filling season. It seems that many years earlier, eleven itinerant workers "tapped" the bottom of a silo on a farm several miles away. The dark liquid of fermented silage flowed from the opening into the drinking cups of the workers. In a likely attempt to find a substitute for hard liquor, they drank it and all suffered and died by the next morning. Although this story has not been verified, it did serve to keep us kids from walking too closely to the silo during those silo-filling days!

Our Silo today.

Chapter 16

The Green Manure Spreader

DAD SAYS I better put on my hat. This will be my first time to ride on our manure spreader and I know that stuff will be flying everywhere! I run quickly outside to the barn where Dad is hooking up the tractor to the spreader. "You may climb onto the seat, but be sure to hang on," he cautions.

Our spreader was painted green and had large metal wheels on the back and small ones on the front. The bed was made of wood and stood about sixteen feet long and four feet wide. Several two-inch angle-iron strips, about three feet long each, were bolted at regular

Better wear a hat!

intervals across the width of a continuous canvas belt. As the belt moved, it carried manure to a large rotating wheel with wire prongs at the rear of the spreader.

We stored the spreader next to the fence surrounding the cow pens some distance from the horse pens. During dry weather, we spent many hours using a wide scoop shovel to toss the manure over the fence and onto the spreader. The horse stalls had straw on the floors, so we used pitch forks and carried the manure several feet before tossing it onto the spreader. The smell was distinct, but not overpowering.

Perhaps the most sensitive part of the process was estimating the degree of "dryness" of the manure. If it were too moist, it was difficult to distribute with the spreader's rotating wire prongs; if too dry, it clogged up the rotating mechanism. I recall a number of times, both in the pens and in pastures, finding "cow chips" that had been dried by the sun and were very hard. Dad explained to me that the early pioneers used them for fuel and that they burned very clean. I picked one up on several occasions and gave it a toss. Years later, I find that many county fairs across the country have cow chip tossing competitions with entries from all over the world. There are no rules on how they may be thrown, so styles can range from a normal baseball toss, to a Frisbee toss, or even a discus throw. Perhaps if I would have pursued that venue, I would be throwing the discus today rather than the javelin.

Of course farming was the main interest and most of the cow chips found their way to the manure spreader. With time permitting, and with a full spreader, we often traveled to our alfalfa fields to spread the manure. Occasionally, though, we stopped for a short time to spread some of the manure over our much smaller cucumber site. It was believed that cucumber growing was greatly assisted by this treatment.

The only time in my memory when we used our horses, other than plowing, was to pull our manure spreader. This was an easy assignment for our horses and I believe that Dad thought it was a chance to give them some good exercise without too much strain.

We started on one end of the field and carefully lined up a direct path to the far side. Dad engaged the lever to start the canvas belt and the rotating wire wheel. Manure was then flung onto the surrounding fields. Instantly, flakes of manure started flying from the back and sides of the spreader. I remember also that some were propelled to the front where we were sitting and hit us directly on the back, shoulders and head. I knew then why Dad insisted on my turning up my collar and wearing a hat!

Compared to today's high-tech farming, using all kinds of fertilizers, pesticides and genetic engineering, I wonder if our "organic" farming might still have been healthier.

Chapter 17

Flintstones and Birdpoints

"AND THEN WE knelt down and found six arrowheads all in one pile," Gilbert said. Boy, is this exciting! Real Indians used to live close to where we live now. Maybe someday soon, I will be big enough to go with them on their next trip to find arrowheads. If I find one, I will take it to Sunday school and show it to the other kids.

Because of uncertain footing for both animals and humans, walking across the farmland required a steady awareness of the contour and geology of the fields. Outcrops of limestone and sandstone dominated the landscape, and rocks of other types often showed up on gentle hillsides, on animal paths and roadways. The unusual rock most often found was flintstone, and its amazing characteristics were great fun to demonstrate. I remember Dad taking two chunks of flintstone into a dark room with my sister and me. He struck one rock against the other resulting in an electric spark jumping several inches. We had no previous experience with this kind of experiment, so the effect was exciting. Dad struck the rocks several times before turning on the light and asked us to the smell the rocks. We had smelled black powder from numerous hunting trips with our parents. So, when we smelled the rocks for the first time, we were surprised that they smelled exactly like the smoke from a rifle shot. Years later, the mechanism for

Birdpoint, Arrowhead and Awl

this odor was explained in a geology class as a typical chemical reaction within flint and brought back pleasant memories.

But, the discovery of flintstones at the foot of the Flint Hills was not the only cause for excitement among kids and adults. From my earliest memories on the farm, the sight of arrow points, ax blades and scraping knives carefully placed on window-sills and dresser tops is very prominent. The land on which our farm rested had been hunting grounds for the Osage, Pawnee, Kansa and Wichita tribes for thousands of years.

Flint was among the hardest minerals known at that time, and it was a logical choice for native Indians to use for crafting tools and weapons. Finding an arrowhead was cause for excitement. In fact, collections would be compared and counts of findings were kept by most families as these finds were treasured by all.

Each cousin, at one time or another, built bows and arrows from green tree limbs. By tying a string from one end of a bent limb to the other and allowing the limb to dry, a workable bow could be constructed. We normally used a knife to sharpen one end of a straight tree branch to make arrows. In an attempt to make a straight flight, we secured chicken feathers to the tail of the arrow. These arrows were satisfactory for target practice, but would seldom fly straight enough to kill any game.

When our cousins visited the farm on weekends, some of the kids convinced their parents to give them an arrowhead called a birdpoint to make a long, straight and deadly arrow. Finding just the right tree branch might take a few hours; binding it with an arrowhead became the next challenge. We cut a half-inch slit at one end of the branch, and squeezed the tail end of the arrowhead into it. With a strand of wet fishing string wrapped tightly around the slit, the arrowhead would become rather stable when the string dried. Then it was ready to take to the field for some bird hunting.

We tried to hunt birds that were considered worthy of a serious hunt. Game birds such as ducks, geese and doves were the most likely target. Our parents never worried when we built the special arrows. But when we succeeded in killing a few birds, they would warn us of the many dangers of the razor-sharp flint arrowheads.

Although we shot at many game birds over the years, I specifically recall only one kill. An older cousin, Sonny, hit a dove sitting on a telephone line. The flopping bird and arrow fell pathetically to the ground with a thump. We ran up and found the arrow had impaled the bird, but the flint arrowhead had turned in its mount and was barely attached. The sight of the kill seemed so repulsive to several of us that we only wanted to shoot arrows at paper targets. The practice of archery soon became more competitive and rewarding as a new-found pastime. Later, as an adult living in Wyoming, I joined an archery club using life-size targets of many big-game animals, but I could never agree to a full bow hunt for live animals. However, I continue to admire and respect flint arrowheads as parts of beautiful collections displayed on shelves and in display cases. In fact, I still have a few of the original arrowheads found on our farm as well as several others purchased over the years from nearby antique stores.

Chapter 18

The Windmill and the Stock Tank

AS I AWAKEN, it feels so cold even under my blankets. I reach over for my water glass—it's frozen. Oh, no! That means we will have to break up the ice in the stock tank this morning.

Much of typical farm life centered around the windmill. Its primary purpose was to supply water to a large stock tank for cattle, horses and other farm animals. In many cases, it was also the only source of our own drinking water, so its reliability was critical and almost daily attention was required to assure its smooth operation. On most days, either Dad or Pop walked to the creek some fifty yards down the hill to the east of our farm house carrying an oil-can for squeaks and a wrench to keep nuts and bolts properly tightened. I remember on several occasions finding them sitting on the edge of the windmill platform smoking a cigarette and staring at the creek nearby—a welcomed pause in a hectic day on the farm.

Water came from two sources: the hand-dug well near the front of our house, and the windmill pumping water up the hill to the stock tank near the barn. The well near the house was dug around 1885, shortly after the house was built. It supplied drinking water for the family until about 1913 when run-off from nearby cow lots started to make it unsafe. At that time, in the late fall, the creek below the hill

Our Lifeline

became nearly dry. One day, when Pop was walking along the creek bank, he noticed a muddy area and over the next several days found the mud to be increasing. He built a wooden enclosure to capture some of the free water and the cattle soon found it a safe place to drink. He concluded that a spring was feeding the area and decided to dig for it. With the help of several neighbors, a solid sandstone shelf was found about twelve feet deep. Clear water soon bubbled over the sandstone to a depth of several inches. A windmill was immediately constructed over the new well providing an excellent source of drinking water for the family and the farm animals. A hand-pump was positioned directly over the base at the center of the windmill. When drinking water for the house was needed, a simple half-inch bolt connecting the main-windmill shaft to the pump was disconnected thereby freeing the hand-pump for direct access to the water below.

After several years, neighboring wells either became contaminated or dried up. Pop invited them to use his well to pump drinking water for their home use. It was soon apparent that the well was not sufficient for the six or seven families and it was decided to dig the well deeper in hopes of finding a greater supply. After hours of pounding heavy metal rods onto the sandstone shelf, it finally broke free. Then after digging another three feet, fresh water carrying fine sand particles streamed in through cracks in the lower shelf. This was a signal that they had struck a good source of water. For years, families from the surrounding area used this well to supply their drinking water needs.

Also, during that time, a narrow, fenced runway allowed livestock to walk up and down the hill from their pens in the barnyard to the windmill stock tank for water. While I was on the farm, Dad and Pop laid a pipeline up the hill and into a new stock tank providing water directly to the animals in the pens.

We believed that drinking water pumped by hand directly from the windmill would be of better quality than that pumped up the hill into the stock tank. So, we pumped several buckets of water and carried them up the hill for use in our house. This sometimes required two or three trips a day and was a very disagreeable duty. Most often, we kids were assigned to this task; carrying only partially-filled buckets, it seemed to take a large part of the day. Years later, long after we left the farm, pipes were laid from the windmill upwards to the hill and directly into the house. An added storage tank provided a more stable water supply.

Winds in the area varied greatly. During unfortunate times with no wind, water requirements for our livestock had to be provided by the hand pump. This required the attention of all members of the family.

We took turns hand-pumping water, but we kids had only the strength and perseverance to pump for a few minutes. The adults appreciated some rest time, and seemed grateful for our small contributions.

A long-handled tin dipper hung from a wire at one side of the windmill. If there were any pleasure associated with hand-pumping water, it was the occasional drink of very cold water from the dipper. A far cry from the bottled water of today, the enjoyment of having pumped the water could not be matched.

The stock tank captured hundreds of gallons of fresh water for the animals, but wintertime posed unique problems. After a few days of below-freezing temperatures, water in the tank formed ice several inches thick. This required breaking it with a large, sixteen-pound sledge hammer. Dad was the only member of the family who could swing such a weight. However, I was given a small hammer to break up the large chunks of ice so the cattle could get to the water. They rushed to the stock tank with steaming breaths to gulp the ice cold water. The look in their eyes was reward enough for that tough job.

Eventually the water under the windmill became contaminated with alkali and was dismantled. My uncle drilled a water-well near the house and, with a new water heater, provided full indoor plumbing for the first time. The windmill, not including the lower-pump mechanism, was reassembled in the yard near the farm house. Today it stands proudly as a reminder of those one-hundred years of service to the farm residents and to thousands of farm animals.

Chapter 19

A Shave and a Haircut, Two Bits

"MOM, LOOK AT this candy jar. It's only a penny for two pieces,"
I shout. "No, it costs too much," Mom says. "Maybe next time."

From my earliest memory, perhaps the most often repeated phrase
I heard was, "It costs too much." Both of my parents were children during the First World War and were married during the Great
Depression. By the time my sister and I were born, the financial condition of our family was severe.

Although the average annual income across the country was about
$2,000, living off the land of the family farm earned a cash-income
of only a few hundred dollars a year. We sold chickens, eggs, milk,
cream, grains, and a few head of cattle or pigs. Most of the resulting
cash was reinvested in seeds for the next harvest and in new-born
farm animals to raise for the next sale.

Some essential supplies, though, were purchased from grocery
stores in nearby towns: a postage stamp cost three cents, although we
seldom sent letters; a half-gallon of honey cost seventy-five cents;
syrup was one dollar a gallon; sugar, thirty cents for five pounds; flour,
twenty-five cents for five pounds; soap, seven cents a bar or three bars
for nineteen cents. These were regularly on the list of supplementary
foods and supplies. Coffee beans were purchased for twenty cents a

pound and were hand ground at home. Other items—including smoking tobacco, paper for rolling cigarettes, and liquid starch and bluing for laundry—were near necessities.

Mom prided herself in "finishing" many of the family's clothes with starch. To this day, I find it hard to believe that Mom starched men's work overalls after each wash. Years later, Mom said that the pride shown by both Dad and Pop was worth her considerable effort and expense of starching and ironing their work clothes. In addition, the collars and sleeves of Dad's and Pop's white shirts were dipped into liquid starch, sprinkled with water and rolled up with other white clothes in a folded sheet or a large dish towel made from a flour sack. They were not ironed until at least a full day later. This dormant period allowed the clothes to become uniformly moistened and made ironing easier.

Before the start of World War II, gasoline was eleven cents a gallon. I recall Dad walking into the kitchen and slumping into a chair, folding his arms and declaring to no one in particular, "Gas just went up a penny a gallon!" Gas prices would raise another nickel a gallon as the war progressed, and each penny increase caused great alarm to farmers in the area.

To cut down on expenses, we did everything we could do ourselves, including cutting hair. My first trip to a barber was not until I left the farm in the late 1940s. Hair care for both men and women on the farm involved cooperation between family members, friends and relatives. Mothers and daughters quickly learned the techniques required to style hair for the rigors of heavy work in the home and in the field. Men were often particular with their hair cuts, but young boys' hair was cut uniformly. A towel was wrapped around the neck and a cereal bowl was fitted snugly over the head, tilted toward the back and just over the ears. Chrome-colored hand clippers were used to trim the hair near the skin, below the bowl. When all the hair was removed, the bowl was lifted and scissors were then used to thin out the remaining hair on top. The expression, "bowl-headed young men" was often used to describe the appearance of farm boys of the day.

For very special occasions, such as weddings and funerals, men on the farm traveled to town to see a real barber. Hot towels, wrapped over their faces and neck, softened their whiskers for a close, straight-edge razor shave. This, along with a careful hair cut, cost fifty cents, or, using an old American term, four bits. A bit signified one-eighth of a dollar, or twelve and a half cents.

In those days, a classic ending to musical pieces performed on a piano, guitar or violin, and sung along by the audience, was a rhythmic "a shave and a hair-cut, two bits." After finishing a violin solo for the family, Dad happily sang and played a newer version, "a shave and a hair-cut, four bits." Then he grinned as he said, "Prices just keep going up."

Chapter 20

Chicken Disease

OH, NO! TODAY is clean-out-the-chicken-house day. Dad hands me a small shovel and shows me how to lift the droppings out the door and onto the manure spreader. "I know it is not fun, but you still have to do it," Dad says.

As a child, my job was to shovel manure out of the chicken house, the horse stalls, the milk barn and the barnyard. I was not the only one—farm kids spent a great amount of time doing jobs that were not really heavy, but time-consuming for parents and other adults. None of these jobs were pleasant, but chicken manure bothered me the most. I tossed shovels full of the dry, dusty waste at my target—a manure spreader or a small box wagon. After only a few minutes of work the chicken coop filled with thick, white dust that seemed to hang in the air. Sunlight diminished as it entered the enclosure.

After several hours scooping chicken manure, I felt flushed and would start to sneeze and cough. Although the general smell of the barnyard was not offensive, certain field smells such as wheat and blowing hay or straw caused the same reaction. At times these reactions were serious enough to cause my nose to drain in a steady flow rather than the usual dripping.

"Ken, I asked you to come back to my office because we found some rather disturbing shadows on your lung x-ray," Dr. Araas said. I had just moved to Wyoming in the fall of 1966 to begin what was to become a twenty-six year teaching assignment at Sheridan College. Because I had no symptoms and was simply fulfilling my obligation for a yearly physical, the doctor's words hit me hard. How could such a health problem be happening so suddenly?

After almost a week of waiting in agony, other doctors were consulted who concluded that my lung shadows showed residual scars from a childhood disease called histoplasmosis.

Though they had rarely seen this disease while practicing in northern Wyoming, the doctors reassured me that it was no cause for alarm. While researching the disease, I found that symptoms include a runny nose, a slight temperature, and coughing. Although I had all the classic symptoms, it would have been impossible for an untrained eye to determine the difference between "chicken disease" and the hay-fever and asthma with which doctors had diagnosed me when I lived on the farm.

In fact, the only way our family knew if someone had a temperature was to hold the back of their hand on the forehead trying to detect any unusual heat. Mom was especially good at this. Even years later, after we had purchased a thermometer, she still used this hand technique to determine fever. Although I may have shown the symptoms, including unusual fatigue, my histoplasmosis went undetected until moving from Kansas.

Today, I am somehow able to reflect on those long-ago times with considerable fondness rather than remembering the harshness of many of our jobs and duties. And I still share what is expected on x-rays with new doctors and well-meaning technicians who become unnecessarily disturbed when first observing my lung x-rays.

Chapter 21

Popcorn Balls

WE HAVE ALREADY had supper and our chores are done. The sun is really hot out here. Dad told me this morning that I did not have to hoe in the cornfield if I would hoe the popcorn tonight. I guess I can pretend that it is a cold winter night when we will get to eat popcorn.

We planted our plot of popcorn each year just to the west of our farmhouse. As a youngster, it seemed like a big field. But when I stepped it off years later, I found it only measured about 20 feet by 40 feet. Eight hundred square feet provided a full supply of popcorn for many winter evenings, and supplied homemade popcorn balls during many yearly holidays. Christmas season was always the highlight.

We popped the corn over an open fire on the wood-burning kitchen stove. A basket made of heavy wire with a sliding metal lid, and a long wire handle with a wooden grip made up the popcorn popper. Mom and Dad occasionally allowed us kids to pop at the stove, but it resulted in burned corn and lots of smoke. My mother maintained that she preferred the burned kernels. She also favored burned or dark toast. Perhaps growing up in a family of ten brothers and sisters helped to develop this taste—it likely guaranteed a better share of the

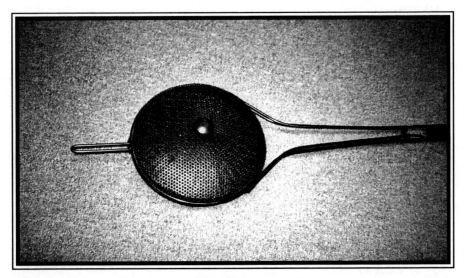

The Popper

food. Dad, also from a large family, showed a similar tendency with a preference for the neck of fried chickens!

To satisfy our family of five, we sometimes popped as many as five batches of popcorn in one evening. Once popped, it was dumped into a dishpan and, using a large wooden spoon, mixed with a cup of melted butter and salt.

We had no paper plates and only a few dishes, so we grabbed a few handfuls of popcorn from the dishpan and placed them on an old newspaper. We sat around the kitchen table with only a kerosene lamp to light the room. With chores completed, and with no electricity or media noise, this was a cozy, quiet and special time for the whole family. Conversation was hushed and generally centered around school and church activities, problems we might have on the farm, and news from relatives. What a vivid time in my memory!

When Thanksgiving and Christmas approached, Mom would look ahead on the calendar and find a Saturday when a few of my cousins, Bonnie and I were at home to prepare dozens of popcorn balls. This was an exciting time for us kids. With an advanced notice of a week or two, a day of popcorn balls was a subject of great anticipation. We were not allowed to actually pop the corn, but we knew we would be directly involved in the final product!

A syrup mixture simmered on the stove nearby a large dishpan nearly filled with about twenty cups of popped corn. Years later, my 90-year old mother shared her recipe: two cups of sugar, one cup of water, one teaspoon of vinegar, one-half teaspoon of salt, and one-half cup of Karo white syrup. These were stirred over heat until the mixture started to boil. A small sample of the liquid was then dropped into water and, if it formed a solid ball, the mixture was declared ready and removed from the heat. After stirring in one teaspoon of vanilla, and, depending on the season, a few drops of food coloring, the mixture was poured over the popcorn in the dishpan and mixed with a wooden spoon.

We kids had the most exciting time! We were now invited to help make the balls. I do not clearly remember having to wash our hands, but now, so many years later, would doubt that we washed our hands very carefully. We then buttered our hands from soft clumps of butter and scooped up our first handful of the mix. With the sticky syrup stirred in, we could easily form a popcorn ball about three inches in diameter. After the first ball or two was completed, our hands became as sticky as the corn. So we dipped our hands into a pail of cold water before forming the next few balls. The job finally required us to dip our hands into water before each ball was made. After several balls were lined up on wax paper, the excitement wore off and our primary objective turned to eating one of these tasty creations. I remember these early samples as being very warm and chewy. Once cooled, the balls were wrapped in wax paper and stored in the pantry. They were shared with relatives over the holiday season, and my sister and I were allowed at least one popcorn ball each day until they were gone. Perhaps only homemade ice cream in the summer tasted as good as these colorful popcorn balls!

The Freezer

Chapter 22

I AWAKEN AND feel the hot summer air all around me. Then I hear Dad smashing ice. I quickly put on my overalls to run downstairs and outside the kitchen door. Dad swings his ax down on the gunnysack containing a big block of ice. He looks up, smiles and says, "We are having homemade ice cream today!"

Ice cream on a summer day continues to be a significant memory from childhood. The hand-cranked freezer furnished a gallon of ice cream with each completed batch. If we had a few visitors later in the day, together we could easily consume a full gallon. If more ice cream was needed, Mom telephoned the visitors and asked them to bring along their freezer and some ice. We would generally furnish the eggs, sugar, cream and other ingredients from our home supply. No cooking was involved in this preparation. I often think back to those days when consuming several dozen raw eggs was not considered a health hazard.

We did not have a refrigerator since electricity was not available on our farm, so we used an icebox to keep food safe. This required getting ice a few times each week. In early summer, ice was delivered to country homes by truck from nearby Olpe. It came in twenty-five, fifty and one-hundred pound blocks. On delivery days, we would hang a sign near our mailbox with the desired size of the ice blocks designated by a printed number at the top. In addition to the three different weight selections on each of three edges, a fourth edge with a "no" showing at the top signaled the iceman that we did not need ice that day. When ice was delivered, the iceman traveled up the lane to the house and knocked on the door. If everyone was in the fields, he entered and lifted the block into the icebox himself. Mom left the ice money on the table to be picked up in our absence. I think back to occasionally meeting the iceman and recall his steady optimism and sense of humor, even though he sold the ice at a price of only about a half-cent per pound.

With the arrival of this special "ice cream day," our first priority was to crush enough ice to pack around the canister holding the ice-cream mixture. Dad placed a 10 or 15 pound chunk of ice into a gunny sack, and used the flat side of an ax to smash it into pieces small enough to fit around the canister. We layered salt into the freezer with the crushed ice to absorb heat from the ice-cream mix so it would freeze faster. We usually purchased the ice-cream salt from the hardware store in Olpe, although, sometimes, we chipped pieces from cattle salt blocks in the barnyard.

During the hand-cranking, we continually checked the level of the salt water in the bucket to make sure it would not reach the level of the canister lid. A small hole on one side of the wooden bucket was designed so that the melted salt water leaked out and onto the ground, before it reached the lid level. We used a small stick to poke it clear as small ice chunks blocked the flow. On more than one occasion, however, the hole became clogged with ice and the salt water leaked into the canister ruining the entire batch. What a disappointment!

Even with such great excitement about the finished product, the actual work of hand turning the freezer was extreme — at least by kids' standards. After starting the cranking process, most kids lost their enthusiasm within a few minutes. Then an adult took over and finished the job in well under a half hour. We were invited to try to turn the handle a few more times toward the end of the process. With the contents frozen at the same temperature as the surrounding salt-water mix, the whole system froze in place and finally made it impossible to turn. It was done!

Five or six gallons of ice cream had to be cranked for eighteen uncles and aunts, and up to twenty-nine cousins. I remember visitors would sometimes bring a freezer of ice cream, surrounded by blankets and gunnysacks, along with them to our farm. Uncle Bud and Aunt Sophie occasionally brought a gallon of vanilla ice cream containing sliced peaches. To offer further variety, fresh sliced strawberries might be added to a batch, or several tablespoons of cocoa might be in another canister. These were special treats and the serving size was highly regulated.

In anticipation of completing the freezing, bowls and spoons were placed on the dining room table. This treat was so special that most adults and kids would stop whatever they were doing, find a shady spot on the grass and savor every bite.

The mothers and the kids tried to keep track of whose turn it was to lick the paddle—an enormous privilege. With all the tiny holes in the metal and wooden paddle, it took some time to lick the whole thing. Trying to eat the melting ice cream on the paddle was a problem, at that a messy one, but the reward was worth it.

At the end of the day, only the empty ice cream containers and freezers remained. We cleaned the metal containers with boiling water, and we dumped the saltwater mix out of the wooden buckets. Generally, we had a specific location for this dumping since the saltwater killed grass and other vegetation.

Then, with nighttime approaching, we could only look forward to the beginning of another hot workday the next morning. But the memory of ice cream would be on our minds for as many days as we had to suffer before once again hearing the exciting sounds of crushing ice!

Chapter 23

Snow Ice Cream

No two alike.

BONNIE AND I stare out the window as we stand near our pot-bellied stove. "I saw a snowflake, Mom, I saw a snowflake!" Bonnie shouts. With a broad smile, Mom rushes in from the kitchen and joins us. "Yes, I see one, too," she says. "This is the second snow. Can we make ice cream tonight?" I ask. "No, not tonight. Maybe by morning there will be enough snow. We will just have to wait and see," Mom replies.

Once harvesting season ended, it seemed that homemade ice cream season also ended. With school starting and heavy work in the fields, time was too limited to make special treats—until the snowfalls began. Then, ice cream made from snow became a topic of discussion at the dinner table and plans were made to prepare this special treat. For many farm kids in the 1930s and 40s, snow ice cream was a highlight of early winter.

Whether a valid belief or not, most families considered the first snowfall of the season as the one which "sifted dust and dirt from the air." Perhaps having clean air to breath after the dirt and grime of harvest season was the dream of all families, and the first snowfall was a good dividing point.

Once a snowfall was deep enough to gather easily, a dishpan-size container was often used to collect the snow. With many animals roaming outside, "yellow snow" was carefully avoided. The deepest and cleanest drift was found and the top layers were scraped off exposing clean, white snow beneath.

After the pan of snow was carried into the kitchen, we gathered around the table to watch the glorious mixture evolve. With a large spoon, Mom slowly stirred in about a quart of fresh cream, a full cup of sugar and a tablespoon of vanilla. The mixture took on a creamy texture similar to the soft ice cream of today. Just as we did with summer ice cream, Bonnie and I argued over who would get to lick the mixing spoon.

This treat could not be scheduled for a dessert because the ice cream melted rather quickly and, with no freezer to store any leftovers, the full amount had to be consumed immediately. Although hard ice kernels as large as grains of sand, along with some dust particles, were sometimes found in the mixture, we did not hesitate to attack the full sample.

Well before the batch of ice cream was ready to eat, the family found their respective dish and spoon. We did not have matching dishes or silverware. Each one of us had a hand-me-down plate, bowl, glass, fork, spoon and knife which were unique and easy to spot in the kitchen cabinet.

This gathering around the table, most often in the late evening, was a delightful time for the whole family. The number of actual snow ice cream feasts likely numbered less than a dozen during my time on the farm; however, they were times of pure joy. For me, in this modern age, a trip to the local ice cream store still rekindles thoughts of the first winter snow and Mom stirring the creamy mix.

Part Two

Learning From the Animals

*As I watched, listened and looked
into their eyes, farm animals around
me taught lifelong lessons of
patience, dignity and oneness with
the universe.*

Chapter 24

Ducks Across the Moon

HERE COMES DAD, running into the kitchen. "Quick, come outside! You have to see this!" Bonnie and I have our pajamas on. What is going on out there that we have to go out into the cold?

Ducks flying south were an inspiring fall event. The first flock we saw in the evening or morning sky brought a shout for all to hear. "Look at all those ducks—what a beautiful sight!"

During daylight hours, a flock passing overhead provided a break in our work that might last a minute or two. At times with only one formation in the sky, we watched carefully the movement of the individual members of the flock. The lead bird, at the point of the characteristic "V" formation, sometimes gave way to another, faster bird before dropping several spots toward the rear of the formation. We figured the lead duck's duty was the most difficult and exhausting. It had to break through the air providing, in today's terminology, "drag" for the ducks following along either leg of the "V."

At other times, detailed observation was a little more difficult with the sky "filled" with a dozen or more flocks, each in a separate formation. This visual splendor of thousands of ducks or geese was accentuated by the "quacking" or "honking" sounds that made it difficult for observers on the ground to communicate. As special as these daytime sights were, catching a nighttime flight of ducks or geese became a lifelong memory.

When Dad rushed into the house one late fall evening, nature was providing a perfect confluence of events. The full moon had risen about two hours previously and shone high in the eastern sky. The view of the sky to the southeast from our farmyard was free of trees and offered an unobstructed view of the full moon on this night. As we rushed outside, the noise from thousands of ducks and geese roared in our ears. I recall the lead duck of a large formation entering the yellow disk of the full moon, followed by an ever-widening span of its companions. Within seconds a perfect "V" shone across the moon's disk. This was followed by another "V," and then another. In the meantime, if we looked carefully away from the moon, we saw dozens of formations visible in the moonlight, filling the rest of the sky.

After perhaps a half-hour, the number of formations gradually decreased until we concluded that the major part of the fly-by was nearing an end and it was time for bed. As we walked into the house, Dad explained that with such good weather, ducks and geese would continue to fly over us and not land in area ponds or in our fields. Perhaps this might not be a good duck-hunting year. This put a slight damper on the evening's excitement; still, the memory of the sky "black" with flying ducks is easy to bring back.

Chapter 25

Culling

DAD FINISHES HIS supper. He starts to get up and then sits down again saying, "We are going to sell some chickens and have some money when I get back from Olpe tomorrow. There must be at least ten chickens that are not laying eggs. Kenny, you can help me pick them out at the chicken house."

Dad had planned on this day for several weeks. He had talked to neighbors and others at church, and had even read an article in our weekly newspaper on the art of culling chickens. The idea was to identify and remove non-laying hens from our flock of about sixty. There are many modern culling methods today that are nearly fool-proof, but during those times, lifting the chicken by its feet and palpi-tating the egg-laying area by hand supposedly found evidence of eggs yet to be laid. This was to be accomplished as the bird frantically flapped its wings and struggled to get free. By culling and separat-ing the unproductive hens the evening before they were to be sold, a check for eggs the next morning confirmed whether or not the proce-dure was successful.

Two screened boxes—about three feet on a side—were used to transfer poor laying hens to market. We carried these boxes to the chicken coop and prepared to capture and cull the chickens, one by one. Dad snared each chicken by a single leg, using a long wire with a hook on one end. He quickly pulled the chicken close, dropped the wire, and held the chicken by its feet. My contribution was to retrieve the wire from the very dusty dirt floor after each capture.

Working our way through the flock caused greater and greater alarm as the chickens frantically tried to escape. Although the enclosure was partially screened, heavy dust soon filled the coop, and I remember starting to cough and sneeze. Finally, we picked about ten chickens as non-layers and placed each into one of the two boxes for an overnight stay. Dad said that the chickens would quiet down after we left, but I remember being quite disturbed at their plight when they were crammed into the boxes.

The next morning, I was awakened by loud laughter from my parents in the kitchen. Bonnie and I ran downstairs to find out what the excitement was. Dad said he had just returned from the chicken house where he was going to load up the culled chickens for the trip to Olpe. When he lifted the crates, he found a total of eight or more eggs rolling around the bottom. Although very much disappointed, he quickly assessed the matter and released all the chickens to join the rest of the flock outside. His disappointment quickly changed to amusement realizing that his culling technique had absolutely no credibility. In fact, it had the opposite outcome than the one for which he was searching.

For many weeks following, Dad shared his story and became a local hero to neighbors and relatives sharing their own versions of the story. After I grew well into adulthood, I still heard the story on occasion, sometimes from a distant acquaintance of our family who had heard it years before. After finding out I was Frank's son, and with a twinkle in their eyes and a slight smile, they would start, "Did you ever hear about your dad culling chickens…?"

Chapter 26

Calving

"STAND RIGHT HERE and do not look in until I tell you. I have to be very careful or we might lose both of them," Dad says. We have waited for a long time for the new calf. I was supposed to see my first calf being born, but now I have to wait behind this wall.

Many calves were born during my years on the farm, with most of them arriving unassisted. But on one occasion the mother cow had several difficult days before the birth actually started. Very early in the morning, before starting chores, Dad had found the mother laboring on the straw-covered dirt floor of one of our small, sheltered pens. Although he had earlier decided that this might be a good time for me to observe the birth of a farm animal, the difficulty of the mother required that I stay out of sight, for fear of frightening her.

After several minutes of tenseness and loud noises from the mother cow, Dad let out a whoop and the calf was delivered into the world. Dad would later tell me that the calf had twisted one of its legs in the birth canal and that it took some serious effort to reach in and straighten the leg for a successful delivery. The calf immediately started to bawl loudly, and the mother struggled to her feet. Dad then asked me to join him in the stall. Although assured by Dad that the sight was quite natural, I was astonished to watch the mother as she cleaned up the birth area. Her strength quickly improved while she worked her way around the stall, and she began to lick the calf to clean it up. Dad assisted with rags and water, rubbing and cleaning the calf.

Within a few minutes, the calf rose up on wobbly front legs and struggled, finally, to rise on all fours. With tentative steps, followed by a trembling body, the calf stood quietly with eyes trying to focus on the surroundings. The mother continued to nuzzle the newborn and gently push it out the opening of the pen and into the sunlight of the barnyard. What a memorable sight! The mother, obviously fatigued, was so caring and attentive. I was spellbound by the whole scene playing before me.

After a few more moments, Dad decided that the situation was stable and we could walk back to the house. I glanced back just in time to see the new calf take a few running steps and kick its back feet into the air before running several more yards. I knew then that this calf would be a friend and I had to figure out a name for it. After several days, I named him "Joey," and observed the appearance of pure joy in his every waking moment. I discovered this new life to be one of genuine bliss, watching as he romped with his mother in the warm, green fields.

As the months went by, Joey and I became close friends. I helped to wean him and watched him grow to a healthy yearling. After my tearful pleading, Dad allowed Joey to live with us an additional year as my farm companion. Then, near the end of the second year, he was herded with the yearlings to market. Later, after several discussions with my dad, I was convinced of the necessity to release him, but have always remembered him.

I realized years later that, although the very purpose for the existence of these animals is to provide food for humans, their short stay on earth reflected nature's way to be immersed in life. What being could be a greater member of the universal order than these lively, energetic and friendly creatures?!

Chapter 27

Calf Riding

*"LLOYD, LET'S TRY to ride Junior," shouts Herman. We climb
the fence and sit on the top board. Looking at Junior across the lot,
he looks awfully big. We have never been to a rodeo, but our uncles
tell us that they ride bucking horses and bulls. Maybe this won't be
so hard!*

In anticipation of a steer providing us with a year's beef supply,
my family chose a frisky Hereford calf early in the spring. We named
him Junior, fed him a special diet and limited his movement and physical activity. This "fattening up" process also required that he be held
in a small pen for eight to ten months before butchering. Day after
day, the kids fed mixed grains and water to the animal. A kind of
friendship generally developed with the calf, and the temptation to
conduct a rodeo was on our minds. Final plans were made and two of
my cousins and I decided to give it a try.

To this day, I remember the incredible strength and warmth of
Junior as I jumped on his back from the nearby wooden fence. I
grabbed the hair on the back of his neck and held on for dear life—
we used no ropes or straps. At first the calf was docile; but, an instant later, he took off at a full, bucking gallop—whirling around the
15-foot, square pen. I quickly found myself on the ground, got up

and ran back to the safety of the fence. My cousins were howling with delight, and lined up for their turn.

It took some time for Junior to calm down, but eventually he walked near enough for Lloyd to jump on. His ride was no longer than mine, but he limped slightly when he rose from the ground and staggered his way to the fence. Herman decided not to go for a ride that day. But for the next several days, we visited Junior and all rode him many times. We learned a little more each time and were finally able to stay on his back for probably four or five seconds. This time span seemed much longer, though, because our heads and noses would sometimes touch or crash into the back of Junior's head while he bucked. His hard spine jarred us painfully, when we bounced from his back and returned with a jolt to our sitting position.

Although weeks went by, we did not notice that the calf had grown into a sizeable steer! On occasion, Junior would not move at all when we jumped on his back. So, one late summer day, Herman grabbed Junior's tail and gave it a twist just as I jumped on. The 750-pound steer let out a snort and quickly moved sideways crashing into the fence and trapping my leg. It took some time to get free. Afterward, I was very sore from my hip to my ankle.

When I took a bath the next Saturday night, Mom noticed a large black and blue bruise along the side of my thigh and leg and demanded an explanation. I finally told her that we had been riding Junior. She was terribly frightened and scolded me fiercely, telling me not to do it again. So ended our playing rodeo, although we occasionally sneaked into pens to ride hogs. They were not nearly as fast or dangerous as steers, although, years later, we found that pigs could bite and severely injure people. We really had been lucky!

As a father, I often considered my own experiences as a child when trying to determine the degree of danger facing my children. With football, baseball, hockey, skateboarding, and even bike riding, the possibility for injury is found everywhere. As kids, we had no helmets, gloves, masks, hip pads, or arm or leg guards: we were bare-footed, wearing only bib overalls. Yet, we somehow survived!

During my twenty-six years living in Sheridan, Wyoming, I regularly watched rodeos presented by National Rodeo Association professionals, high-schoolers and youth groups. Kids as young as three years old ride sheep in "Mutton Bustin" competition. With sheep weighing up to 200 pounds or more, this can be an exciting time for both kids and their parents. When youngsters get a little older, calf riding and roping, barrel racing, and horse racing are added options.

Ready to play.

Questions of cruelty to the animals and the possibility of severe injuries to the participants are expressed whenever these events are staged. In my day, animals were respected and offered great fun and excitement. The thought of their ultimate destiny in the slaughterhouse never entered our minds; instead, we found these bovine friends our constant companions during their brief stay on the farm. The memory of their bright eyes, stamina and dignity remain with me to this day.

Chapter 28

On Horseback

THE SUN IS shining brightly and the birds are singing from near-by trees. This might be a good day to ride a horse. I hardly ever get to. "Can I ride a horse today?" "Maybe after the chores are done," Dad says.

Horseback riding for fun rarely happened on our farm. My parents were pressed for time and seemed perpetually fatigued. The daily grind of farm work left little time for recreation or outside activity. Other than church on Sunday, our playtime was carefully rationed.

Horses on our farm were primarily used to pull plows, wagons and other equipment. On rare occasions though, when we were very young, Dad lifted us to the back of a horse and led it around the barn-yard. This was great fun, but soon we wanted to control the animal ourselves by riding bareback. We found a rope, wrapped it around the neck of our horse and climbed onto its back. At first we found this a difficult task until we learned to lead the horse to a nearby wooden fence. This "ladder" gave us a way to climb to the height of the horse's back before jumping on.

We knew from watching western movies in Olpe that the Indians always rode bareback, and did it very well. When we tried to gallop on our horse, however, we found it painful bouncing up and down on the hard backbone. We figured that our legs were not long enough to keep from bouncing and we could not hold ourselves firmly to the horse without losing our grip. So we longed for a chance to ride on a regular saddle with a bridle. We found out quickly, however, that this was a luxury allowed only on very special occasions.

On a Saturday morning with no pressing farm duties, Dad and I herded my favorite horse into the barn. Spot seemed to know that this would be a special day and pranced to the bench that held the saddle. I stood back while Dad retrieved the bridle and reins from a nearby hook. Spot raised his head and momentarily bared his teeth before opening his mouth to receive the bridle bit. His eyes sparkled and he began a little dance, alternately lifting one foot and then another. After tying the reins to the saddle bench, Dad hoisted the saddle onto Spot's back.

Spot was easy to saddle. He sucked in his stomach as Dad pulled tightly on the saddle-cinch belts. Dad said that when Spot was very young, he purposely swelled his stomach so that it would loosen later. The rider would then find a loose saddle shortly after starting the ride. This dangerous experience was not often repeated. Dad checked and double-checked the straps, and if he found the horse was not cooperating, he would either strike its stomach with his closed fist or with the side of his boot. Then, almost in the same motion, he pulled tightly on the straps. This felt uncomfortable to the horse—and it likely learned the lesson, quickly.

At first, I rode up and down the long drive that led from our house to the country road. When I looked back toward the house, I saw Mom watching anxiously from the kitchen door. This fear seemed unfounded to me, but many years later I found out why she felt that way.

At the age of ninety, on one of many road trips to the home place, Mom shared a story with me that she carried with her since she was

16 years old. We had driven past a certain corner many times over the years. But on this day she pointed to the red barn and said that she had her first date with a seventeen-year old boy who had lived there. A week after their date, the young man was bucked from his horse and died of a broken neck. She spoke sadly of how that experience had frightened her whenever one of her family rode a horse.

During my sophomore year in high school, my family moved to a cattle ranch near Saffordville, Kansas. My father was hired as the ranch foreman, and I had the opportunity to help him and started riding horses more seriously. Our main duties were during daylight hours, but when it came time to send the cattle to market we spent several days and evenings rounding up cattle from the pasturelands.

I convinced Dad that I would like to spend a night under the stars near the cattle—just like in the movies. He approved of my idea and that night became a memorable one. Using my horse's saddle as my pillow and his blanket for cover, the nighttime quiet of the prairie gradually turned into nighttime whispers from the past. The mix of smells from horse and saddle leather took me back to those days when my friend Spot brightened my young life and created a lifelong memory.

Chapter 29

Slopping the Hogs

"YOU CAN HAVE some cookies as long as you eat them over the slop bucket," Aunt Sophie insists. Darrell and I eagerly grab the warm oatmeal cookies from the rack beside the stove. We are very careful not to get crumbs on the floor. It is difficult to lean over the bucket without bumping our heads against each other. Tonight I will help carry this slop bucket to feed my favorite pig, Earnie.

The slop bucket had a life of its own. Early each morning the bucket was carried in from the small porch area just outside the kitchen door. It was placed on the floor near the kitchen stove and, with no sink or running water, became the all-purpose drain and garbage disposal.

Two large dishpans, half-filled with water from the outside well, were heated on the wood-burning stove early each day. Starting with coffee grounds in the morning, everything—except bones—was scraped from dirty dishes into the 5-gallon bucket. The bones were tossed outside for the dogs to chew on. The dishes soaked in the hot water along with a little homemade lye soap. After washing and drying the dishes, the left-over soapy dishwater was tossed onto the yard outside the porch door. Potato and other vegetable peelings and cores, especially during canning season, were added to the slop bucket. Water left over from cooking—and other garbage accumulation—nearly filled the bucket by the end of each day.

As part of the evening chores, we carried the bucket to the pigpen to "slop the hogs." During the hot summer months, water was allowed to overflow from one side of the stock tank onto a fenced hog-wallow area. I recall the absolute delight shown by our hogs as they rooted through the fresh mud while cool water slowly streamed into the pit. As many as a dozen hogs at one time occupied the enclosure. At one end of the pen, we built a long, wooden feeding trough where we poured their food.

We stored farm-grown, ground-up corn, wheat and other grains, as well as store-bought bran, in a safe place in the barn away from rats and mice. These grains were mixed with the slop, and then dumped over the wire fence into the pig troughs. The troughs were placed next to the fence so that the pigs could be fed without anyone entering the pen. I liked doing this because it made the hogs so happy. The squealing, grunting and clamoring for the food was a sight to behold. Some of the smaller, more agile pigs jumped into the trough to get an eating advantage. Rather than fight the unavoidable, we simply poured the slop directly over the pigs while they ate and drank at the trough. They seemed to laugh, as they grunted, and eagerly licked each other's ears and heads and continued to root around in the trough. When they finished their trough food, we threw a few small buckets of corn on the cob into a dry area of their pens. They rushed over and, with a front foot on one end of the ear of corn, bit off and crunched the hard kernels with an intensity heard all the way to the house some 50 yards away. Eventually the feeding frenzy diminished and the pigs stretched out in the cool mud and snoozed through the night.

As a precaution, we looked for erosion near the fence line which might allow the pigs to escape. Hogs are notorious for rooting through soft ground, and the prospect of chasing them back into the pen compared with the vision of "herding cats!" But, occasionally, they did manage to get under the fence. In addition to repairing the damage, we sometimes took the escape as a signal to clamp heavy, copper rings into the noses of the more aggressive pigs. This required a special pair of pliers to force the wire into the flesh between their nostrils. This procedure caused quite a commotion with lots of squeals and panic from the pigs, but helped greatly to curtail rooting under the fence. Even then, we often found them with noses bleeding after rooting so hard that they tore the rings from their noses. Others were quite docile, and would even come to the fence to have their ears and head scratched.

Most farm animals, including pigs, show individual personalities. After a full summer watching their barnyard behaviors, it was often difficult to let them go to the market in the fall. My favorite pig,

Slopping the hogs.

Earnie, was allowed to stay an extra year before selling at a very high price during the following season. In fact, Dad allowed Bonnie and me to each start a saving account at the Olpe bank from the profits from Earnie's sale.

Although the hogs lived in filthy conditions, it never occurred to me that those conditions could hinder our great delight in eating pork chops, pickled pigs feet, bacon, sausage and other delicacies they provided.

Chapter 30

Skunk Hunting

"MOM, COME HERE, quick! Shep is really acting crazy." I run over to him and he whines and rubs his nose in the dirt. Mom comes running with a bucket of water and splashes it over my dog's head. Then she dries him off with a rag. Boy, he still smells awful!

The thrill of the forthcoming skunk-hunting season is still with me—even after 60 years. Dad said we had to wait until cool weather "set in," so that the harvested furs would be "prime," and have proper texture and thickness to sell.

Although many of the animals we hunted, such as muskrats, were found near water, skunks could be found anywhere—under a rock, or under or in an old barn. But usually we found them in the pastures. They lived in holes dug in the ground and their tunnels often stretched for a hundred feet or more with sharp turns.

On a particular day, after a rain, Dad asked my cousin Lloyd and me to go down near the windmill by the creek and dig for some night crawlers. Bullhead fishing was so much better with these long, thick earthworms than with the regular skinny worms found here and there over the farmland. Furthermore, a single night crawler could be pulled apart into two or three pieces, multiplying their usefulness.

We were kneeling down in a muddy area picking up worms when we looked up to see two tiny, bright black eyes looking at us through the surrounding tall grass. My cousin and I froze, as did the large black and white skunk! Before we could decide on an action plan, the skunk turned and let out a spray that stopped time as it flashed toward us. We ended up with bright, yellow "goo" on our clothes, face and neck. We ran to the house screaming and slapping at the sickening spray. We knew that our only hope was to get help from Mom. When she heard us approach, she grabbed some warm water and soap from the kitchen. While we stood outside, she helped take off our clothes and washed us down. It was impossible to get the stink out of the clothes, but with intense scrubbing, we finally cleaned our skin. I will always remember that day and still, when I pause to reflect on it, can almost bring back to my memory that unique and awful smell.

My skunk hunting experience with my dad primarily involved conventional trapping methods along the creek. But on occasion we searched for them by either hiding out near the chicken house at night or trying to find them near our old barn. When we or our dogs did come across a skunk, we would be careful not to get into the way of their awful smelling defensive spray. Each of us, however, at one time or another, got into the skunks' line of fire. Our success at harvesting skunks probably averaged only three or four each season.

Our neighbor to the south, Ralph Jones, on the other hand, was famous throughout the area as the best skunk hunter in the county. One time he told us a story of going on a skunk hunt. To start the adventure, he went to an old, abandoned chicken house to retrieve his "skunk hunting clothes." They consisted of old overalls, shirt, jacket and rubber boots. These clothes were never used except for the hunt because they had a permanent stink. He then got a digging spade, a stout club and a 12-foot length of barbed wire. The wire was clipped just short of a barb and used to "twist" into the skunk's fur before dragging it out of its lair. He then saddled his horse and headed out.

Traveling over the pasture, he looked for the opening of a den that might contain skunks. He also hoped to see small hopping bugs, similar to gnats. If these were found, it was almost a sure thing that a skunk was at home in the den. It seems that skunks were a favorite host for these bugs. Then, Ralph spaded the tunnel opening to get to the main level. He inserted the barbed wire into the hole and twisted. He had no luck on this try. More digging followed, and a turn in the tunnel was found. Again, he tried the wire, and on this occasion found four skunks in one den. After pulling a skunk out, he hit it on the head with the club and stuffed it into a burlap bag or sack. On at least half of his hunting trips a skunk would turn its rear toward Ralph, sending the potent spray toward him and onto his clothes and skin.

The main clearing-house for purchasing the skins was the Lyon Fur Company in Kansas City, Missouri. They quoted prices for different kinds of skunks. Black was the most desired followed in value by short stripe, narrow and, finally, broad stripe, which had the least value. Black furs brought the most value because it had finer fur than the coarser white. In all his years, Ralph never found a pure black skunk, but he did catch several with short stripes.

Finding and killing skunks was not done only for the fur. Skinned carcasses made good bait for other varmints. Ralph often suspended a carcass a few feet above the ground, and setting a trap under it, caught possums and other skunks almost every night.

Ralph often told a story about a one-room schoolteacher who stayed at his home. From his position in a shed on one side of her path, Ralph stretched a long piece of twine to an un-skinned skunk that he hid on the opposite side in a nearby bush. He waited until she walked by and he gave it a yank. A terrific scream followed and she almost fainted from fright. After recovering, they both enthusiastically shared the story for years after.

My fondest memory of skunks was on a summer day when I walked the long path to the mailbox. Suddenly, just a few feet ahead, a mother skunk and four tiny babies strolled directly in front of me. The little ones followed as closely as possible behind that terrible tail. How ironic that their protection was our fright!

Chapter 31

MY DOG, PAL and I are running near the barn. I'm hearing a very loud buzzing sound coming from the creek down below the hill. We have just finished dinner. Why are those katy-dids making so much noise this early in the afternoon?

On each summer afternoon, cicadas (we called them katy-dids—others called them locusts) started their cyclic harmony at unpredictable times. Perhaps temperature, humidity or some other factor determined when they would join the chirp of a single leader and then suddenly build up into a loud symphony.

One summer evening Dad and I were walking near the creek with one of our dogs. Pal especially enjoyed these walks since he anticipated the usual encounters with these loud, flying insects. Numerous cicadas flew in and out of the timber. Pal lunged after them—biting into the air as they flew near the ground. He finally nabbed one. He closed his mouth around the insect and tried to work his tongue around it to either chew or swallow it. He rolled his head from side to side and danced around in circles, then suddenly stopped in bewilderment: the bug was gone.

Within seconds, he began looking down at his stomach, frantically swinging his head from side to side. Then he stopped, slowly

Pal's Buzzer

tilting his head back and forth with his ears perked up, intently listening to a buzzing sound coming from his stomach. It was so loud Dad and I also heard the sound. We watched in awe as a memorable show began.

As if chasing his tail, Pal ran around in a small circle for a few seconds, stopping to listen at his stomach, and then resumed his circles. He took off in a straight line for several yards, kicking up his back feet as calves and horses often do. With a quick stop, tilting his head to one side and then the other, he lay down and aggressively started biting his stomach. In frustration, he made muffled growling sounds. He rose up and frantically continued rushing back and forth past Dad and me. After what seemed like several minutes, and many more passes, Pal gradually slowed down and the buzzing finally stopped. For the rest of the evening, and even during the next day, Pal paced the site sniffing the ground and the air. I would imagine he wondered what had just happened to him.

Pal and I later walked the creek many more times, but never again did he capture the elusive cicada. It is likely that many dogs have captured many cicadas, but Dad and I must be among the very few to be so thoroughly entertained by such a spectacle.

Chapter 32

Weaning Max

"WE WILL START weaning Max tonight," Dad said. I already did a good job with Bud, so I know this will be a fun time.

After several weeks being fed by its mother, a calf finally reaches the stage of eating on its own. To accomplish this weaning process, the calf is removed from the mother and put in separate corrals so that it can first take milk from a bucket and then gradually begin eating solid foods like oats and other grains. The first few nights of separation are traumatic both for the animals and for the farmers. I remember many nights awakening to hear the bleating of the mother cow, sometimes followed by the cry of the young calf. If two or more calves were being weaned at the same time, the night would likely be filled with bawling sounds. These cries made me sad and it was difficult to get back to sleep.

The first step in weaning is to teach the calf how to drink milk from a bucket. After separating the cream from the fresh milk, I caught a bucket of the remaining skim milk and carried it to the corral housing the young calf.

By petting Max and talking to him several days before the weaning process, the calf knew me and came running to meet me on the important, first evening. I lifted the bucket over the fence and tried to tempt him by placing it directly under his mouth.

On rare occasions, a calf might immediately suck the milk into his mouth, but at other times they needed a little assistance. I held the bucket in my left hand and sprinkled drops of milk on his nose and mouth with my right hand. This did not work with Max, so I dipped my whole hand into the milk and placed one finger near his mouth. He saw the finger bathed in milk as a teat and started sucking on it. The tongue felt rough as sandpaper and sometimes it was difficult to remove my finger from his mouth. Alternating different fingers eventually got Max to start searching for more milk, finally finding a full meal in the bucket. This took about two or three sessions. Of course, with more than one calf to wean, it took considerable effort to supply buckets of milk each evening during the weaning process.

After I left the farm, buckets were manufactured with rubber nipples attached near the bottom, making weaning a much easier process. But I think of all the young kids who missed out on an enlightening experience after the invention of the new bucket.

The closeness developed while weaning carried throughout the growth of our calves. Most of the calves were named at birth by Mom, Bonnie or me, and we continued to follow them during that first year as they grew to market weight. During that time a calf might be chosen to become food for our own family. It was then placed in a small pen to "fatten up" before butchering. My cousins and I visited and fed them in the pen and occasionally tried to ride them bareback.

These short encounters invariably helped develop a bond, and as the calf grew on its eventual path to our icebox or the market, there was often a reconnection and a hesitation to sell or butcher it. Terrible feelings erupted when I thought of them going to their death. It was as if my dog was to be killed. My sister often wept and I fought hard not to cry. But, finally, with a quick scratching on the top of his head and between his ears, and a final meeting of our eyes, I would say goodbye once again to a temporary friend.

Chapter 33

"DAD, PLEASE LET me go coyote hunting with you tomorrow."
"Oh, OK. I guess you can go this once, but you are really going to
have to stay close to me the whole time," he says. Mom frowns and
looks worried.

My one and only coyote hunt took place on a Sunday afternoon
in the late fall. For several weeks, dinner table conversation centered
around plans for the biggest hunt in memory. The coyote population
had steadily increased throughout the late spring and early fall. On
many farms in the area, coyotes killed calves and other small farm
animals—and we had to reduce this threat.

Although most hunts covered a three-section land area of three
square miles, this one was to cover four sections. The land area was
chosen with the owners' permission because it was clear of trees, had
very few small bushes and was on rather level ground. About a mile
north of our farm, this site included our little one-room schoolhouse,
Stony Ridge, on the southwest corner.

Each of the four sides of the area had a captain. Each captain was
responsible for recruiting hunters to safely cover the "walking line."
Normally, this numbered about 6 hunters per mile. On this day about
25 walkers lined up on each side for a total of 100 people making up

the hunt. Men, women and older children took part, and each hoped he or she would kill at least one coyote.

For safety, no rifles were used, but a few shotguns with light loads were allowed along the line. Generally, a single shotgun or two at each corner was considered safe and proved helpful at the early stages of the hunt.

An exact time of the general hunt was determined. On this day it was one o'clock p.m. The head captain fired a shotgun ten minutes before the start to signal three or four hunters at each corner to slowly walk diagonally toward the center of the hunting area. At each corner a hunter fired a few shots into the air to force any coyotes near the starting lines to run away toward the center of the hunting area. This helped keep them from quickly escaping through the line. After the corner hunters advanced some distance, taking about 10 minutes, the remaining hunters in each line started their slow inward walk. They carried clubs and sticks to kill coyotes that might escape the loop.

In some of the earlier hunts, horse riders were allowed in the line. Some of the fences along the way were damaged by the horses and not repaired. This aggravated the landowners and they demanded that no riders be permitted on this hunt. But, toward the end of our hunt, a lone rider decided to ride in and kill the coyotes. Almost immediately after breaking the line, his horse caught a load of buckshot from an unknown shooter and he quickly changed his mind and retreated from the scene.

I was so excited I could barely contain myself when Dad handed me a heavy hedge pole to carry in the line. Within a few minutes, I saw a number of animals running ahead of us. Dad told me they were jackrabbits. They were much larger than the cottontail rabbits that we regularly hunted and had enormously long ears. They were so fast that it would have required a very good marksman to shoot them on the run. When we did get one though, it made a very good meal, especially in a "pot pie." Shooting, of course, was not permitted on this kind of coyote hunt. The fate of those jackrabbits trapped within our shrinking square was to be the same as the coyotes.

A designated spot had been pre-determined near the center of the hunt as the location of the coyote and jackrabbit harvest. As the walkers came closer, some had to slow down or speed up so all might reach the center at the same time. Up to this point in the hunt, our line had only encountered a few jackrabbits that attempted to escape. We clubbed most of them, and we carried the carcasses to the center meeting point.

Dad and I were almost shoulder-to-shoulder with the other hunters as we walked over a slight rise. What a memorable scene—more than one-hundred jackrabbits and twenty coyotes ran back and forth between the four converging lines. Although a few animals were shot in the early stages of the hunt, all these were killed with clubs. I remember waving my club as the animals approached, but neither Dad nor I were involved in an actual kill. There was a large amount of whistling and shouting to confuse the trapped animals, but several escaped over the last ten minutes of the hunt.

When the hunt was over, nearly one-hundred jackrabbits were laid side by side. The coyotes, also lined up some distance away, totaled eighteen. The rabbits were divided among any hunters who wanted them and the coyotes' ears brought a bounty of two-dollars per pair. Some of the hunters tried to tan the coyote hides and make coats, but Dad said that never worked well.

I will always remember that day! Mom was delighted to see me come back in one piece. The community excitement and recollections of the hunt continued for many months. After that year, the coyote population dropped. I wished I could have picked off some coyotes like the old-timers did!

Chapter 34

Gray Hair Overnight

BONNIE AND I are selling homemade lemonade under the ladder that goes over the pasture fence. Here comes Dad, our only customer. He is walking slowly toward us after making his rounds to the oil wells. He is so tired after fighting that big bull and buck sheep.

During the fall of 1943, Dad was employed as a truck driver and oil-well pumper for an oil company north of Winfield, Kansas. My family and I lived in a company house on the lease surrounded by the wells. From early spring to late fall, both cattle and sheep grazed the pasture containing the wells.

Normally, Dad started his rounds at the break of day to check pumps and start gas engines that may have stopped during the night. This required several miles of walking which he always enjoyed. Although these wells had no high-rise oil derrick overhead, they had a large opening under the well-head called a cellar. Nearby was a fenced slush pond, some 50 feet across, with vegetation growing heavily around it. A 250-barrel, storage tank also stood by each well.

The long years working in the oilfields involved very hard work, but were still rather routine. However, during one two-day period, Dad had a most unusual experience and he loved to tell about it. Over the years, Dad's story became more and more detailed and was one that kids and adults alike found both humorous and spell-binding. He started with the first day of this frightful adventure.

That morning, as Dad unloaded a truckload of oil-field supplies, a large pipe rolled over his left hand and caught the middle finger just above the fingernail, breaking the bone and pulling out the nail. He quickly drove himself to town, some eight miles away, where the company doctor treated the finger and placed it in a cast. With no one else to do the job, and no sick leave allowances, Dad returned with his painful injury to the field that afternoon.

Early the next morning, in a heavy fog, Dad started the rounds earlier than normal, attempting to compensate for being slowed down by the injury. He had just arrived at the first well when he heard a deep bawling and, searching the darkness, barely saw the face and horns of a large bull charging toward him at full speed. Dad ran around the slush pond just ahead of the bull. The bull came to an abrupt stop, changed direction, and came toward him from the other side. Dad could see the bull through the reeds and brush and tried to stay opposite him. After a stand-off period, which seemed like hours, the bull still appeared to have no intention of leaving. Dad formulated an escape plan. He dismissed any attempt to fight off the bull because his finger now throbbed badly. To further complicate the escape, Dad was wearing knee-high, hard-rubber boots. The bull moved one way and then the other around the pond, but could not see Dad's location, and finally stopped. The bull stood in one spot for several minutes. Dad thought that a dry ravine, some 100 yards away, would offer his best chance to begin his escape. He crept toward it on hands and knees, keeping the bull in sight through the grass. Surprisingly, he made it safely to the ravine without the bull seeing him. Dad knew that the bull would not be patient for long and that he had no protection if he were discovered.

Trouble!

Dad felt that a section fence—now in full view, another 100 yards away—was his only hope. He took off at a dead run, not looking back. When he got close to the fence, he flung himself to the ground and rolled under the lowest strand of barbed wire. The bull snorted into the air, as he ran by the fence. Dad lay there exhausted for several minutes—reliving what had been his closest encounter with mortal danger. He was quite sure that it was enough for a lifetime! That afternoon, he called the owner of the bull, who agreed to pen him up for a few days to calm him down.

Next day, in nearly the same spot as the bull encounter, Dad unloaded a truckload of oil-field supplies. A large buck sheep "came out of nowhere," and delivered a crushing blow with his horns to Dad's right hip. He was knocked to the ground and wrestled briefly with the sheep before running to the nearby storage tank. The buck followed close behind. In what seemed like a recurring nightmare, he again found himself in a stand-off position with a very angry animal. There was no escape this time, especially since Dad could not see the buck over the tank. He picked up a one-by six-inch board and a ten-pound, round iron thread protector and decided to attack—even though the pain in his hand was almost unbearable. The buck charged and Dad hit him squarely on the head—barely slowing him down. Each time the buck came toward him, Dad side-stepped, hitting him alternately with the board and the iron ring, while slowly working his way to the safety of a nearby fence. Again he escaped under the fence leaving a very angry buck sheep on the other side.

A few weeks after these events, Dad noticed considerable graying at the temples. Although he lived to be 77 years old, he still had gray hair only at the temples. We have all read about people becoming gray overnight—but I have first hand knowledge of this reality.

Chapter 35

Squirrels and Sputniks

"BEFORE WE GO hunting, you need to learn how to call squirrels," Dad says. Dad reaches into his pocket and hands me two fifty-cent pieces.

My first squirrel hunt was in the fall following my first rabbit hunt the previous winter. Squirrels and rabbits with diseases would likely not survive cold weather, so Dad felt that it would be safer to hunt only after the first freeze in the fall. Sometimes we hunted earlier if the weather had been cool for a few weeks.

Squirrel hunting is considered more dangerous than rabbit hunting, since rifles were most often used instead of short-range shotguns. Dad felt that the line of sight or the prediction of the path of a bullet was more limited in the deep woods as most squirrels are shot from high tree branches. Underbrush and unsure footing were other problems with woods hunting.

The weapon of choice was generally a .22 caliber rifle. Ammunition was chosen from three types of .22 rounds—short, long

Barking Squirrels

or long-rifle. The range of these bullets was from a half-mile to over a mile-and-a-half. Since our targets were in trees, Dad chose the short-range option. On my first hunt, however, I used a single-shot .410 caliber shotgun. This not only made it safer for other hunters, but the wide pattern of the shot made it easier for me to shoot a squirrel. The problem was, of course, that as more shot found the target, more meat would be damaged.

Our hunting area was in groves of oak, walnut and cottonwood trees within a few miles of our farm. Dad and I walked nearly a hundred yards into the woods until we found a fallen log to sit on. After a few quiet moments, he took out a couple of half-dollars and, holding their rims at right angles to each other, struck them together producing a "barking" sound closely resembling that of real squirrels. After a few attempts, he paused, carefully checking the branches of nearby trees for a pair of ears or the bright eyes of a curious squirrel. If the prey came into full view, Dad allowed me to shoot with my shotgun. Other times, if the squirrel froze in its sheltered position, Dad went for a "head shot," seldom missing.

We often stayed in the hunting area for a few hours, occasionally moving several yards to a new position. This provided quiet time which Dad sometimes used to further my hunting education. I could then practice calling squirrels using the two coins and I remember being successful once or twice. Dad asked me to predict where a rifle bullet might land when fired at a particular target. He pointed out tree trunks and limbs behind a target that might deflect or stop a bullet. On the other hand, if clear skies were seen through the branches, we took a chance of shooting another hunter. These lessons served me well during big game hunting years later in Wyoming and Montana.

With four or five "kills" in hand, we headed home to dress and clean the game. Rather than pulling the heads off as we did with rabbits, we took the whole squirrel from the field. Once home, we gutted the animal, and cut the skin behind the head pulling it down past the legs and to the tail. We used a small hatchet or knife to cut the head, tail and paws from the squirrel leaving the carcass ready to quarter and prepare for cooking.

We shook the pieces in flour in a paper sack and then fried them in lard until they were brown on all sides. We then placed them in a pan, covered them with milk and cream and baked them for an hour in the oven of our wood-stove. The resulting white gravy was poured over mashed potatoes or slices of bread.

Once I remember taking a bite of squirrel and having little black pellets fall onto my plate, rolling to one side. This was obviously a squirrel killed with my shotgun!

Years later, after our family moved to town, Dad and I planned an early Saturday morning squirrel-hunting trip a few miles southwest of Emporia. As usual, we left the house an hour or so before sunrise on this October morning—with thermos bottles of coffee and a few snacks. Nestled in an opening near the woods, we shared our thoughts on the world's future while listening to the radio news of the Russian Sputnik space craft launched the previous day. The world-wide excitement was at a high pitch as newscasters described the satellite and its characteristic broadcast-sounds directed to earth. For some reason, Dad reached over and adjusted the radio dial as far as it would go to one side. Almost instantly a "beep, beep" sound filled the air. To have encountered aliens at that moment would not have come as a bigger shock. We were stunned listening for what was probably less than a minute to these sounds that must be coming from the satellite passing overhead.

During the next several days, I shared the experience with my classmates and my physics teachers at Emporia State. They showed interest, but with not nearly the excitement that Dad and I felt on our last early morning squirrel hunt.

Part Three

My farm was my world, but after occasional trips a few miles from home, the complexity of the outside world started a lifelong search into the mysteries of the full universe.

Chapter 36

A Saturday Evening Picture Show

TONIGHT WE GET to go to the show! This is going to be the most exciting evening of the summer. "You need to do everything I tell you today so that we can get there before the show starts," Mom says. My sister and I start to jump around the kitchen. "We'll do anything you want us to," I shout. I think I heard Mom and Dad talking about Ken Maynard as the cowboy in tonight's show.

In all our years on the farm, we went to the picture show in Olpe only a few times. Other than Christmas, those were probably the

most exciting days in our young lives. About every second or third Saturday night, the little town of Olpe would sponsor an outdoor movie shown on an east-west street just off Main Street. The event attracted as many as two hundred people from the surrounding countryside, which was likely a high percentage of all people living in the area. Although a few kids from my Sunday school were in attendance, we were not allowed to "run" with them.

Chores before the picture show.

This was family night, and we stayed together in our seats for the entire evening.

After a day of almost perfect behavior, and with chores done early, Mom, Dad, Pop, my sister and I would climb in the car for the ten-mile trip to Olpe. It was not dark enough to show the movie until after sunset—well after nine o'clock. When we drove in, we saw cars already parked along either side of the three-block long, graveled Main Street, as well as on some of the side streets.

The portable movie screen was set up on the west end of the street, away from the store lights. The organizers for the movie set up folding chairs they borrowed from a local church. A number of people brought chairs from home. Although the total number of chairs was close to two hundred, some people stood or walked around during the show, especially the smokers. To get a front-row seat, however, required arriving two to three hours before show time. A hat was passed around for donations before the movie began. The average family probably tossed a quarter or a fifty-cent piece into the hat. The total donation was enough to continue these outdoor shows for several years.

The shows usually featured such western stars as Tom Mix, Gene Autry, or Ken Maynard (apparently my namesake). Comedy features included Laurel and Hardy or the Three Stooges. My favorite movies, by far, involved cowboys and Indians—featuring scenes with fast running horses and lots of pistol and bow-and-arrow shooting. For kids of that day, it was similar to the popular car chase scenes or the space-ship battles in today's movies.

The novelty of a movie shown on an open-air screen late at night to a few hundred enthralled viewers is an exciting memory. Not until years later, did I first enter an inside theater. Watching color cartoons, a weekly adventure serial and sometimes a double feature in Emporia's Lyric Theater was the best place to be on the occasional

Saturday afternoon. The ticket price was 12 cents and popcorn and a pop were 5 cents each. With a 25 cent allowance, my sister and I then managed to save 3 cents a week for some special purchase. A few years later, we sometimes moved up to the intermediate 15 cent admission at the Strand Theater farther north on Commercial Street and, rarely, to the high-end Granada at the north end of Commercial where admission was 25 cents.

These movies were not rated as they are today. Other than an occasional kiss on the screen, few objections were voiced. Apparently, regular smoking scenes and the killing of cowboys, Indians and "bad" guys was acceptable to that general population. In today's terms, these movies were not "politically correct." We never thought about them as "cowboys good, Indians bad," we were only aware that there was a lot of action that we could day-dream about for all the next week while doing those dreaded chores. The salvation of the movies was that "good guys (cowboys, Indians or whoever) win, bad guys lose." I do recall, a number of times, my mother telling my sister and me that this was "just a movie. Don't get too excited about it." But, we just could not help it!

Chapter 37

Table Manners

"WASH YOUR HANDS, kids. We will be eating dinner in just a few minutes," Mom says. Finally! I am starved. It seems like I haven't eaten for days, although it's been only since breakfast at sunup. Giving our hands a quick dip in the water basin, Bonnie and I run to the kitchen table and sit down. Where is everybody? Pop and Dad come through the door, wash their hands and sit down. Fried chicken, boiled potatoes and beets. What could be better?

With the exception of breakfast, Mom and Dad made a special point that all members of the family sit down together at each meal. In the early morning, family members might have extra chores or early field work requiring breakfast at irregular times. Dinner was the big meal, especially in the summer, on weekends, and during school vacation days. On many occasions we would have neighbors or relatives to help in the fields and they were also included in this noonday meal.

Once seated, Dad would ask one of the kids to say the prayer. We never deviated from the standard, "Come Lord Jesus, be our guest, and let these gifts to us be blessed." Often, when we said the prayer too fast, Dad firmly reminded us that we always needed to be serious when saying our prayers.

Mom walked around the table with a spoon and a bowl or platter filled with food for the meal. She generally knew what our favorite chicken pieces were, so she quickly parceled them around the table. The same was done for the potatoes, followed by a scoop of white gravy for the potatoes or, sometimes, for a slice of bread. Vegetables included green beans, peas, corn, or beets. Rarely did we have a lettuce salad since the growing season was so short and buying it in town was not an option. But, if the vegetables were in season, and a planting survived the rabbits, we occasionally had a creamed lettuce and vinegar dish served alongside our regular meals. The only bread we ate was either a store-bought or homemade loaf. I do not recall rolls of any kind. Everyone at the table drank milk with their meal, although a choice of skim or whole milk was offered. We had dessert regularly, which consisted of homemade cakes, pies and occasionally some kind of fruit dish.

Not only were we expected to arrive at the dinner table on time, we knew that each person at the table would stay in their chairs until everyone completed the meal. There was no exception—unless the necessity of a bathroom break was convincing. We knew little about protocol for passing food around and using silverware. The saying was, "You can reach if you keep both feet on the floor."

Even though everyone at the dinner table was tired from six or more hours of hard labor, we shared a light and cheerful mood. Table talk centered around the work of the morning and our parents attempted to include us kids, asking specific questions about our work morning.

Evening supper was a much simpler meal with soups, cold cuts, leftovers of various kinds, and often fried potatoes and eggs. Sometimes, when Mom had been working in the fields all day, we had a very light snack such as popcorn and apples or pears. This allowed for a more relaxed meal-time and was well accepted.

Salt and pepper shakers were left on the table at all times. We had no napkins of any kind, either paper or cloth! We ate fried chicken and some other foods with our fingers. Soiled hands were wiped on our pants or licked clean!

Mom or an occasional female visitor set and cleared the table. Although many families had special china handed down over generations, our dishes were an assortment of many shapes and colors, some purchased at the general store in Olpe, and some given to us by friends and relatives when they moved.

Early each evening, a large dishpan was half filled with water and heated on our kitchen wood stove. Dirty dishes from the day's meals were carried into the kitchen and stacked on a table or cabinet. Any food remaining on the dishes was scraped into a 5-gallon bucket, later carried to the pig pen. The soiled dishes were then placed into the dishpan of boiling water. Lye soap, often home-made using ashes from wood fires, assisted with the hard-to-clean dishes and pans—but hard scrubbing was the key! The clean dishes were then placed into a second dishpan where boiling water was poured over them, rinsing off the soap. Bonnie and I then helped by drying each dish with a dishtowel before placing them in the cabinet, ready for meals the next day.

Today, television and TV trays have facilitated the demise of the family dinner. Is it enough to have dinner together only at Thanksgiving and Christmas? I feel so fortunate in my youth to have heard conversations relating to home finances, politics, health issues, weather and so many other interesting topics. Each day we lose another chance to connect with our children. We have lost so much as a society!

Chapter 38

Bubble Lights

"KENNY, IT'S TIME for supper," Mom shouts. "Just a moment," I plead. This is the most beautiful sight I have ever seen. The bubbles just keep going up in those tiny glass tubes. I could sit here watching them all day!

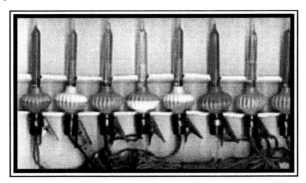

Bubble lights

World War II had just ended. With morning and evening farm chores being the only major obligation during the middle of the winter, a Christmas-time trip was planned to visit Uncle Con, Aunt Hilda, and our four older cousins in Winfield, Kansas. Neighbors agreed to do our daily chores on the farm, and after we attended church services on Christmas Day, we departed on the four-hour trip.

We arrived after dark. Although we had visited Uncle Con's home a few times before, we were startled by the absolute beauty of the inside decorations. Each room had a group of lighted candles, with pine-bough wreaths placed on tables and wall shelves. When we entered the living room, we found a most breathtaking sight: a Christmas tree, standing a full 12 feet high, stretched to the ceiling. Large multi-colored lights formed the tree into a perfect triangle, occupying nearly one full corner of the room.

Although common in modern-day home design, this unusual 1940's living room had an extended, second-story hallway on one side. Glancing upward, I saw my cousins Arlene and Bernita smiling and waving down to us. They seemed to delight in watching Dad, Mom, Bonnie, and me gasp at the magnificent sight.

I found a nearby chair so that I might take in the full beauty of the room, and especially the tree. Although I had not picked up many details at first sight, I observed that not all the lights were the same. Some were bubbling! Perhaps as many as two dozen bulbs had glass stems containing liquid which bubbled and rose to the top of the bulb.

I had many new experiences that evening, including sitting down to a large dining room table that sat ten people. A white tablecloth with matching cloth napkins, along with real silver tableware, was a sight I had never seen. The crystal glasses contained water, with ice! Milk and coffee were usual beverages at mealtime on the farm, but neither was offered this evening until after dessert, when coffee was offered for the adults.

Dinner conversation highlighted Christmas activities and the ending of World War II. Uncle Con quite proudly shared a story about the new Christmas bubble lights. A friend at the local hardware store alerted him to this new invention and saved a set for him. When Uncle Con went by to pick them up, there were three sets of eight bulbs each—and he purchased them all. What an exciting story! I could not wait to get back to the living room to see them. The problem was that in Uncle Con's house, kids had to sit quietly during the entire meal and were not permitted to leave the table until the adults finished their after-dinner coffee. This made for a very long evening and only a little time left for bubble-light watching.

The next morning, new experiences continued. Uncle Con's hunting dog, Lady, was introduced to us. He permitted her to stay in the house on certain occasions—especially during cold weather. Although she was a delightful and friendly dog, we never allowed any dog or cat to enter our house on the farm. Years later, as I think about it, it seems rather contradictory that farmers working around hundreds of animals every day seldom allowed them into their home, and yet, city folks often welcomed them into theirs. We always had a couple of dogs and several cats, but their home was the barn!

Cousins Rolland and Junior led Bonnie and me to the second story of their garage to show us another new and wonderful purchase. There, in the middle of the uncluttered floor, sat a shiny, silver airplane. It was a perfect size for me to climb into and paddle-drive and steer around the loft. After a few turns with my sister, we were, much too soon, led back down the stairway. What an exciting experience! I was the pilot of my very own plane. On subsequent visits, Bonnie and I asked about the little plane, but were never again to drive it.

To make this short visit perhaps the most memorable few days of my first eight years, the Saturday afternoon newspaper arrived at my Uncle's doorstep. I never saw such a rush to the door! Three or four cousins, along with Uncle Con, raced to be the first to read the "funny papers." My uncle, of course, won the privilege. After a short time, my dad showed me what all the excitement was about. There, in full color, was a series of short stories or events depicted in pictures with each comic strip featuring a special hero. It was on that day that I was introduced to Dick Tracy, Blondie, Little Orphan Annie, Barney Google, and my eventual favorite, Denny Dimwit.

The visit ended with an uneventful trip back to the farm. However, over the next several years, dreams of little airplanes and bubble lights regularly continued for me. Recently, I found an old box of eight "bubble lites" in an antique store. I bought them, plugged them in, and they lighted perfectly. Now, as I stare at this year's Christmas tree, my wife calls out, "Kenny, it's time for dinner."

"Just a moment," I plead. I could sit here all day watching those bubble lights!

Chapter 39

An Indoor Toilet

"IT'S TIME TO get up. We are going to Winfield," Mom shouts. It seems like we just went to sleep! Across the bedroom, Bonnie jumps out of bed, shouting excitedly, "We're going on a trip, we're going on a trip!" Mom lights the oil lantern on our dresser so we can see in the dark.

It was late January of a very cold winter. After several postponements, Dad had finally made arrangements with Mom's brother Carl and his wife Clara to do the farm chores in our absence. Grandfather, "Pop," lived with us, but his health limited how much he could do.

For me, this was a major adventure. It marked the second time I had made such a long trip. A few years earlier, during a tornado-filled day, we made the 100-mile trip when moving to the farm from Winfield.

The trip was planned to start at about seven in the morning. Dad and Mom rose early for nearly all of their activities so Bonnie and I knew we would be awakened very early. Sure enough, at about three we heard Mom's call. We dressed and, after a quick, cold breakfast, helped load blankets, pillows, and other supplies into the car. Dad was nervous about the chores, but expressed confidence that Uncle Carl and Aunt Clara would soon arrive. We had left the milk cows in the corral by the barn the night before so they would not have to be herded in from the pasture that morning.

With an average driving speed of about 30 miles per hour, and with several stops along the way, we expected a four or five-hour trip. The air was very cold, but the stars shone brightly in the clear sky. Mom and Dad occupied the front seat, while Bonnie and I sat in the back.

During the trip, Mom carefully explained our expected behavior at meals and at bedtime, as well as the use of the indoor bathroom at Uncle Con's. She described how rolled paper was used rather than our customary catalog paper. Mom said that we should flush the toilet after we were done and that when we were in the bathroom, the door should be closed. Bonnie and I got more worried by the minute. Why are we visiting Uncle Con and Aunt Hilda if we have to be so good, and why do people put stinky toilets inside their house? When we flushed the toilet, where did everything go? We figured out that it would be warm in the house bathroom, unlike our outhouse—which on this morning would have a temperature of about zero degrees.

It seemed like a very long drive; we arrived at mid-morning. After our greeting, the first thing on my mind was finding the bathroom. I asked Mom for permission to use it, and received a "don't start now" look, in reply. Since Mom had visited Uncle Con's several times, and knew where the bathroom was, she finally accompanied me down the hall at one side of the kitchen toward Uncle Con's reading room. She led me in, showed me the lever to flush the toilet, instructed me not to mess up anything, closed the door and left.

There I stood, in the middle of the rather large room with a white sink about chest high on one wall, and a beautiful bathtub along another wall. I quickly stepped up to the tub and looked over the side. It was all white except for brown stains near the drain under a strange silver faucet. I kneeled down to check out the legs of the tub and was

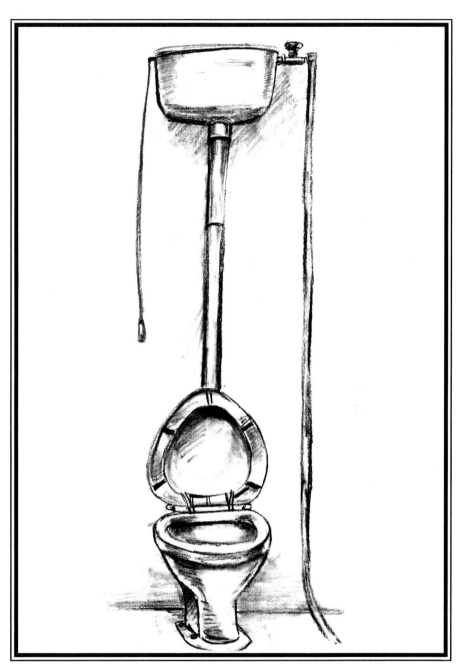

Strange noises.

shocked to see that they looked like the feet or claws of a really, really big chicken. Why would they put those things on a bath tub? I would have to check that out with Dad.

The smell was so unusual. Apparently, there was perfume soap on the trays of the sink and bathtub. Strange rolled paper was mounted on a dispenser near the toilet. I flipped it a few times to get an idea of its use. Although the floor was linoleum, it was covered by several throw rugs. Cloth hand towels hung near the sink. Why would anyone have to wash their hands when living in town? Maybe the towels are here just to look nice, I thought. I had never seen such large towels as those hanging near the bathtub. High on the wall was a little window, opened just a few inches from the bottom. I could see the delicate window curtain fluttering into the room from a gentle, outside breeze.

Strolling back to the toilet, I lifted and lowered the seat several times before finally leaving it up. Knowing that Mom would soon check up on me, I quickly used the toilet. With water already in the toilet I was surprised at the loud sounds coming from the bowl. This gave meaning to the word "tinkle" which I used many years later with my own kids. I wondered if people in the rest of the house were hearing me at that time. I felt embarrassed and I quickly hit the lever as Mom instructed.

With an enormous rush, water swirled into the bowl. I was petrified. Did I break something? Surely everyone heard the disaster. I ran to the door, pushed it open and quickly found Mom. She was talking to Aunt Hilda and showed no concern at all for the gurgling sounds still heard from the end of the hall.

As the day progressed, I heard the flushing sounds coming from the bathroom numerous times, and decided that I would rather get home to use my quiet, comfortable outhouse. At least people would not hear when I used the outdoor toilet.

By the middle of the afternoon the next day, Dad and Mom talked about departing on our trip back to the farm. Dad observed that the weather outside looked more and more like it might begin to snow. We packed up and started our long trip home during the late afternoon.

We traveled north on Highway 77, when ice started to form on the windshield of the car, and Dad became alarmed. We made steady, slow progress, however, and passed the relatively large town of El Dorado. Dad decided to continue heading north to the well-traveled Highway 50. Heavy snow began to fall and Mom instructed us not to say a word in the backseat because the driving demanded Dad's full attention. Mom's voice sounded so concerned that Bonnie and I sat motionless as the trip progressed.

Dad pointed to short metal bars running horizontally across the center of the highway, and he thought they must be there for nights like this. He guided the left front and back tires over the bars and declared that this would be our only hope to make it through the storm without the car sliding into the side ditch. Years later, I found that this 20-mile stretch was an experiment by the highway department to alert drivers who might stray over the center line. Dad maintained that it saved us that night. We finally made it to the small town of Florence just as the road became impassable.

Dad and Mom decided that we would stay that night in our car as the ferocious snowstorm continued. It was beyond what any of us had experienced. After a few hours, Mom and Dad finally tried to find a room in the hotel on the town's main street. This was the first time for me to stay in a room other than my own or that of a relative. Dad left us in the car so that he could ask if a room was available. He returned and, after serious discussion relating to the four-dollar room charge, we all gathered up pillows and blankets and ran through the snow into the hotel lobby. I had never before seen such beautiful ceiling lights and stuffed furniture. After signing in, we got a key and walked up the stairs to the second floor to our room.

Looking around, I asked about the toilet. Someone said it was down the hall past several occupied rooms, and that everyone on the second floor would be using the same one.

The next day broke with clear skies and easy driving on to Emporia and down to our farm south of Olpe. But, what an incredible experience I had that weekend. First, acquainting myself with an indoor toilet—and then using that education to use a bathroom with total strangers in a fancy hotel!

Chapter 40

The Auction Barn

THE COUSINS HAVE just left for home, but this is not like other Sunday evenings. Dad just told me that I could go with him to the cattle auction in Olpe tomorrow night. Since I am eight years old, he said I was finally old enough to stay out until midnight after the sale is over.

Monday night livestock auctions were regular events in the small town of Olpe, about 10 miles east of our farm. Dad had planned for some time to buy two or three calves to add to our small herd. Like most events involving people whom we seldom saw, Dad was particularly nervous to enter the tight quarters of a "Sale Barn" and publicly bid on his choice of livestock.

We finished chores early that evening. Dad and I hurried to the house to wash up and change our clothes. I knew that this would be a truly special evening because Dad dressed in a pair of dress slacks and polished, Sunday shoes. I dressed in my regular overalls and flannel shirt.

On our trip to Olpe, Dad attempted to give me an idea of what to expect. I remember, clearly, his description of the bidding process. He assured me that if I sat quietly with my hands in my lap or on the

bench beside me, I would have no trouble with the crowd or the auctioneer. This was a startling prospect, as I had assumed the experience
would be very entertaining. He told how he made bids by placing his
forefinger to the side of his nose. Dad said that I must listen carefully
to the auctioneer, but I had no idea what was about to transpire.

We arrived well before the 7 p.m. starting time and walked quickly to survey the cattle penned up behind the sale barn. Dad spotted a
few calves that seemed to meet his requirements and made a mental
note to recognize them when they later entered the sale ring.

We walked around to the front door of the barn and entered the
brightly-lit arena. It smelled just like our barn, but that was where the
similarity ended. Gray, wooden bleacher seats rose several rows from
the ground in a full semi-circle around the front of the barn. The dirt
floor was covered with straw and sawdust. A round pen, about thirty
feet across and directly in front of us, had wire fencing about four feet
high. Stretching toward the back on both sides of the pen, a narrow
wire passage opened to the doors of the outside holding pens.

Dad and I took positions to one side about half-way up the bleach-
ers. Dad casually greeted a few members of the crowd and reminded
me, once again, to keep my hands still. He said, "I do not want to buy
an animal that we do not want."

A man strolled out to the front of the ring and announced, "It's
auction time!" A magnificent bull was led into the ring causing a buzz
of excitement to lift from the crowd. "This fine animal comes to us
from the Jones ranch and weighs in at about 1700 pounds. Let's start
the bidding at a hundred..." That was about the last time I understood
anything the auctioneer said. A combination of mumble-jumble and
sing-song sounds continued throughout the evening with pauses just
long enough to bring other animals into the ring. I sat on my hands
and watched as members of the crowd raised their hands or nodded
their heads. I got pretty good at seeing the various bidders make their

wishes known to the auctioneer. Some just winked their eye and others shrugged their shoulders. The auctioneer's assistant shouted out a loud, "Here," as the auctioneer continued his chant. Then another, then another, until, finally, the auctioneer called out, "Sold!" This was the most fun I ever had.

People in the crowd started to leave although the auction continued. Dad whispered to me that it was good to see them go, that way we would have less competition for the calves that we wanted.

Finally, one of our calves filed in. I sat on my hands extra hard as Dad sat upright, ready to make his bid. The auctioneer started his banter and Dad did not move. When the auctioneer was just about to close the bid, Dad placed his finger on the side of his nose and the auctioneer's helper acknowledged Dad's sign. Dad exchanged a number of bids with another customer until, finally, with Dad making the last bid, the auctioneer declared the calf sold. I was so proud to be part of the winning bid and the owner of a new calf. We bought two more calves that evening and left the auction barn after 11 p.m.

On the way home, Dad excitedly talked of other subtleties of the bidding process including people who were placed in the crowd to drive up the price and "phantom bids," where the auctioneer pretends that a bid has been made. He said he did not see any of that this evening. He certainly was an expert in my eyes, and he bought the calves for what he said was a "very good price."

I did not get to bed until after midnight, but it was still hard to go to sleep. The auctioneer said he would deliver our new calves to our farm sometime early in the morning. This was so exciting!

Marker in the Flint Hills.

Chapter 41

Coach Rockne

DAD IS JUST finishing a bottle of beer as we sit at the table. "Kenny, let me tell you about that airplane crash I saw," he says. Now I will hear a good story! "I had been feeding cattle and just came in for dinner…"

The story of the Knute Rockne crash was retold countless times during my childhood. The date of the tragedy was March 31, 1931. Memorizing 3-31-31 has helped me to enrich many conversations over the years.

Several neighbors recalled hearing an airplane in the dense, overcast sky. Dad first heard the news from an older brother when he came in for noontime dinner. The telephone party line rang steadily to alert everyone in the area that a plane had crashed some five miles to the north of Dad's family farm.

Dad first thought that it might have been a mail plane or the kind of small private plane seen occasionally flying over the area. But within the next hour or two, the party lines buzzed with the news that a commercial airplane carrying several passengers had crashed. Dad said he "felt a need" to ride his horse to find the crash site. After dinner, and after completing a few vital chores, he quietly saddled his horse and rode north across the prairie. Although twenty-three years old, he did not tell anyone in his family that he was taking this trip. He felt they would disapprove since he was not in the rescue party and might "get in the way."

Within an hour, he found the crash site. From a distance of several hundred yards, he noticed a number of automobiles parked in the area and several people scurrying around. He easily picked out the plane's tail section lying undamaged several yards from the main wreckage. As he watched the scene for several hours, more automobiles arrived. Some people ran around the area looking for souvenirs. Dad simply described them as looters who prevented an accurate investigation of the cause of the crash. Because the sun started to set, and because chores were on his mind, he rode away from his viewing spot. He recalled that several bodies were collected and taken from the site during that afternoon.

When he came home, he learned that a list of passengers had been released, and that the famous Notre Dame football coach, Knute Rockne, was among them. Dad returned to the area for about an hour each of the next several days and finally made his way to the actual crash site. He described the shards of glass scattered over the area. He picked up a few to take home. Unfortunately they were lost over the years.

The crash had taken a total of eight lives and was the subject of numerous news stories and journalistic descriptions over the next several decades. It caught the attention of both locals and people from other parts of the country. A modest memorial was eventually constructed, along with a wooden rail around the memorial to protect it from grazing cattle. Since the site is on private property, and some distance from the paved highway, it is difficult to travel there. However, on special anniversaries, the landowner opens the memorial to the public and provides transportation and guidance for those interested in a first-hand visit.

On the 65th anniversary of the crash, March 31, 1996, I drove from Topeka to the little school-community house in Dad's hometown of Bazaar, Kansas. That was to be my first visit to the site of the many stories Dad told me about that fateful day. On the clear, cold, windy day, approximately fifty people showed up at the 9 a.m. meeting time. We were briefly informed that several SUV's would take everyone to the site. While warming up in the school house, I surveyed a number of newspaper clippings and bought a little clay cast replica of the memorial. We then began the thirty-minute drive up the hill. I happened to sit next to Michael, a young and energetic reporter for the *Emporia Gazette*. He was very cordial and I shared with him some of the "Knute Rockne crash" stories from my father. He showed great interest and took a few notes with the intention of developing a representative story for the day. Upon arrival at the site we streamed out of the cars. I was struck by the silent beauty of the surroundings. Everyone's mood was solemn, yet excited.

We gathered around the granite and limestone memorial. Cattle had used the guardrails to rub against and had worn away the soil around them. After a short prayer, a representative from Notre Dame made a few kind remarks about Mr. Rockne and the other seven killed in the tragic accident. Several members of the victims' families placed flowers on the memorial. At almost the exact moment of the crash—10:47 a.m.—a single-engine plane flew over our heads from north to south. The hum of its engines was the only sound of the moment. With the brief ceremonies completed, several members of the party started the return trip to the school. The rest of us remained to walk the area. I looked out to the west, between two gentle mounds, to try to imagine exactly where my dad would have been on that day. When the last vehicle was about to leave, Michael joined me for a few final moments at the scene. I saw him smile as he looked over my shoulder to the west. He said, "Look out there!" I turned around and felt a chill as I saw a lone rider resting his elbow on the saddle horn and, with no movement whatsoever, staring directly at us. We saw his cowboy hat, but could not recognize any other details. He was at the exact spot I had imagined Dad to be 65 years earlier. "What an incredible coincidence," I gasped. We both looked at each other, neither saying a word. Our trip down the hill was nearly silent as each passenger had his own thoughts of the day. The drive back to Topeka was very pleasant. My mind was filled with memories of Dad and a feeling of his presence.

Chapter 42

Corn Picking and Selling

"MOM, HOW MUCH longer do we have to stay in town?" I ask. "We only have to stop at two more houses, and then we can head home," Mom says.

In mid-summer on the farm, sweet corn was a source of much needed income for our family. Although we sold eggs, chickens, milk and cream to a store in nearby Olpe, we sold sweet corn from door to door in the south end of Emporia, some 20 miles away.

We anticipated our first day's trip for several weeks. Very early in the spring, we prepared a site within the confines of one of our regular corn fields, and several rows in from the edge of the field. Secrecy was necessary since a sweet corn crop spotted from a nearby road tempted those who passed along the field. It was not uncommon to have a full crop of sweet corn stolen during nighttime. The plot was "worked" by hand with a hoe and rake to create a smooth, inviting surface. Once ready to accept new sweet corn seeds, we planted by hand with deliberate care, having saved the seeds from the previous year or purchased from the feed store in Olpe.

A sweet corn crop was much more expensive than field corn, but we gambled on our ability to grow and sell extra "roasting ears" in town. The term, "roasting ears," was a carryover from the pioneers

who buried them in hot coals. That technique evolved in the early 20th
century to simply mean boiling in water until ready to eat. This was
a time of great anticipation and renewal after a long winter. Maybe
we would have a super crop and lots of town customers this summer.
With dollar signs as a motivator, we tended the small area late into the
early summer evenings—this was after a full day's work in the fields
and in the barnyard. Good rains and warm days sometimes produced
as many as 50 dozen ears of corn to sell for either ten cents a dozen
or a penny per ear.

After chores in the early morning, Mom, Bonnie and I filled gunny sacks and bushel baskets with bundles of six ears of corn wrapped
with binding twine. We loaded as many as ten sacks and bushel baskets into the trunk and the back seat of our car. The trip to Emporia
seemed extra long as Bonnie and I sat on the sacks. However, because
seat belts were not yet invented for automobiles, we had some mobil-
ity to change positions in the car.

After arriving in Emporia, Mom parked the car along the curb
and, carrying several bundles of sweet corn, walked from house-to-
house knocking on the doors and offering the corn for sale. On many
occasions, she came back at the car to replenish her supply before
continuing up the street. In the meantime, Bonnie and I sat in the car
for what seemed like hours. We did not read books or play games.
The only excitement was an occasional car or truck passing by or a
person walking on a nearby sidewalk. On other days, Mom had little
or no luck in selling, and we rode back home quite discouraged. The
next day, however, might provide renewed enthusiasm and I remember we often sold all the corn that we had available.

After the sweet corn season passed, field corn was next on the list.
As with all ears of corn that might be "roasted," edibility was determined by pressing a thumbnail into one of an ear's kernels. If "milk"
squirted out, the ear was good. Late in the season, with sweet corn

gone, Mom or Dad checked the field corn ears for "milk" in hopes of finding a few that might be edible.

Preparation of roasting ears of sweet corn was quite simple. We added ears to a pan of slow-boiling water, one at a time. It was important to keep the temperature of the water at a constant boiling point for two or three minutes. Cooking field corn, however, was a more difficult challenge. This tougher corn required more boiling time: up to twenty minutes. Mom sometimes added a teaspoon of sugar to sweeten the ears.

I did not find field corn at all tasty. Mom and Dad most likely pretended to like it as it was the only alternative so late in the season. Today, even with sweet corn available throughout most of the summer, and with microwave cooking making it an easy meal, memories of those long-ago days still linger. Just imagine—after preparing the field, controlling weed and pests, praying for rain and finally driving over forty miles each day for several days, we might have a total income of five dollars. Added to this was Mom's incredible courage and fortitude to knock on the doors of strangers to help provide a basic survival for her family. I must share this story with my grandkids!

Chapter 43

Bridges and Railroad Tracks

"DON'T EVER DO that again! What were you doing so near a train in the first place?" Mom shouts.

A visit to Pop's new house in Emporia was an exciting prospect. First of all, it provided a rare chance to go into town, and secondly, several cousins would be there as playmates.

Pop had just moved from the farm to a little house just south of the railroad tracks on State Street. A small living room, kitchen and bedroom allowed almost no room for visitors, so we kids were "chased" outside. Pop's yard was also very small, so finding something to do and a place to do it was a challenge. By the second visit to Pop's house, my cousins and I found an easy path leading to the railroad tracks.

As we walked along the tracks, Larry retold a story he heard about placing a penny on the tracks to be run over by a train. What a great idea! Lloyd almost immediately produced a penny and carefully laid it on a track. The feeling of "on the edge" adventure sent chills through us as we heard a train approaching from the distance. We quickly ran from the track to a hiding place near some brush several yards away.

Perhaps because I was only seven, a fear crept in that maybe the train would derail and crash, and we would all have caused serious trouble. Before we could change our minds however, the steam engine of a freight train roared by. With wide eyes, I am sure, we all watched for several minutes as the train continued to rumble past. Finally, the caboose chugged by and the train disappeared. Trembling with excitement, we crawled back up to the tracks and stared with wonder at the flattened penny still laying on the tracks—exactly where we had placed it. Edgar carefully picked it up—it was still round, but well over an inch in diameter. It was so thin that it showed a couple of tiny holes. What pure joy!

We could not contain ourselves as we ran back to show the adults our experiment. Our excitement was not shared by our parents, however; instead they were upset because of our proximity to a fast-moving train. We lost most of our enthusiasm for this "penny activity," but not for railroad tracks and trains.

Several months later, a number of cousins again collected at Pop's place and decided once more to walk the tracks—this time to try to find a railroad bridge described to us by other kids. Cousin Herman joined our pack as we started our trek. Finally, we saw the bridge in the distance. After sprinting for several minutes, the full bridge came into view. As we got closer, it seemed to grow larger and larger until we were standing at its opening. The bridge towered over us, but it was just wide enough for a train to pass through.

We were old enough to realize that if a train rolled toward us on the tracks, there would be no room for anyone to stand on the bridge. After a very brief discussion, we decided that we could run the bridge span before a train would get there—especially if we knew it was coming. We had been told by our older cousin, Don, that if we knelt down and put one ear on the track, we could hear the rumbling of an approaching train from many miles away.

Everyone listened but heard nothing as we started across the bridge. At first, the narrow spacing between the ties offered a view of a concrete ramp some three feet below. However, within a few yards the ramp dropped away to the river, running several feet lower than the ramp. After a sudden breath of fright, we nervously stepped from one tie to another and made it across the bridge. We could not have crossed more than a few minutes when we heard the roar of a train and its whistle. We hurried down the embankment at the side of the tracks and into the high grass. Within seconds, the train sped by with a burst of noise and wind that thrilled us all.

How could we not have heard the train's approach? Years later, I tried listening to the tracks and found it to be quite easy to predict a train was on the way—especially in the summer time when the rails expanded making a tighter contact. Perhaps, as kids, these ventures were during the late fall or winter when the cooler contracting rails left more space between them and less chance for sound to travel through them.

I swore never to try a railroad-bridge crossing again, although some of my companions suggested that we crawl under the tracks and sit on the concrete ledge while a train passed. I loudly voiced my opposition and suggested that we head home. A few of the others said they would come back later to try the new idea. To my knowledge, they never did. Looking back at those days of coal-fired engines, might the trains have discharged super-hot steam just as they crossed the bridge? If any of us had been caught in the steam as we sat on the ledge below the tracks, we would have been scalded; it would have been a terrible tragedy!

Chapter 44

Doodlebug

MOM SAYS WE have to get up at three tomorrow morning to take Dad to the train in Emporia. So we have to go to bed early. I have never been close to a train before. I know I can't sleep.

Dad's older brother, Conrad, lived in Winfield, Kansas, about one-hundred miles south of our farm. Visits were very few over the years and, if the whole family made the trip, we drove in our car. Since only Dad was traveling this time, the train was cheaper, and, he hoped, much less stressful, than driving.

We were up well before 3 a.m. on that very exciting, fall day. Dad dressed in his Sunday white shirt, brown slacks and polished brown shoes. He nervously smoked a cigarette and paced the kitchen floor while Mom checked the final packing of his suitcase. Bonnie and I carried pillows and blankets to the car for the twenty-mile trip to Emporia. Once underway, we were too excited to sleep as we listened to Mom and Dad talk about the adventure ahead.

It was still very dark when we arrived. I had imagined that the depot would be bustling with activity. However, only a few sleepy people, including a couple of soldiers, were waiting near the ticket booth. (In those days, we called all military personnel, "soldiers.") A single light bulb hanging from the ceiling was the only light. In our present time, this might have been a scary setting, but it represented the norm for bus and train stations in the little towns across America during the early 1940s.

After what seemed to be a very long wait, we heard a shrill whistle in the distance and knew Dad's train ride on what was called the Doodlebug was near. The name Doodlebug has an uncertain origin as it relates to a train. But, an insect does exist by that name and, as it walks in soft dirt, it leaves a characteristic winding track. To doodle, then, is to meander and certainly this little train meandered throughout the countryside of our nation during those war years.

Bonnie and I stepped up onto a wooden seat and looked out the dirty window. A puff-puff of heavy black smoke erupted from the train engine, and the train squeaked to a stop. With a further lurch, the engine spewed white steam from both sides near the front wheels.

The passengers and other people in the depot filed out the single door to board the train. A conductor stepped from the passenger car door and invited the travelers to step forward with their tickets. Dad gave us a nervous smile and turned and walked to the train. Two or three other passengers joined him, stepped up a couple of metal steps and disappeared into the passenger car.

We saw Dad through the open windows as he walked down the aisle to his seat. He was apparently too self-conscious to look at us from inside the train so Mom suggested that we walk back to the car for the drive home.

Three days later, we traveled back to Emporia to get Dad from the train station, but this time in the afternoon. Dad looked grim as he stepped from the train; something was wrong. He was wearing the same white, long-sleeved shirt that he wore on the trip to Winfield, but dirt and grime had been added.

A regular traveler on the Doodlebug might have anticipated open windows on the passenger cars and the heavy, black engine smoke which found its way into the cars and onto the passengers. This came as a surprise to Dad. On the way to Winfield during the nighttime trip, the windows were closed, but on this very warm day, the windows had to be opened to offset the stifling heat.

Dad calmed down after a few minutes and escorted Bonnie and me to check out the train. We saw that the engine was constructed in tandem with the single passenger car. Directly behind the engine was a compartment for carrying mail and small freight. The train occasionally carried livestock including chickens, sheep, pigs and calves. Dad said that the passenger compartment could seat up to thirty people. The conductor told Dad that the train could reach a speed of 65 mph, but with frequent stops, seldom did.

Many towns along the original route of the Doodlebug are very small. It is difficult to imagine that Madison, about ten miles south of Olpe, served as a "hub" for Doodlebugs. Trains would split directions there, with some going toward destinations in southeastern Kansas and others traveling southwest to Winfield before continuing into Oklahoma and Texas.

Smokin'.

Steam engines, which required frequent stops for water and coal, gave way to diesel engines which could travel long distances without stopping. This, along with affordable air travel, contributed to the death of many small towns. Lonesome segments of railroad tracks may still be found near ghost towns along old Doodlebug routes.

Chapter 45

The Iron Lung and the Stone Man

"WE WILL BE leaving for town in a few minutes," Mom says. It has been a long time since we went to Emporia. Polio is really scary and we have to be careful not to get too close to people. They might give us polio. Mom said we should be safe as long as we walk on the street and are not in the stores very long.

This would probably be the most frightening day of my young life. The trip to town was uneventful and we found a parking place on Commercial Street around Third Avenue. School would begin in a few weeks and my parents wanted my sister and me to "start out right" with a box of crayons, a writing tablet, a new dress for Bonnie and a pair of jeans for me.

We left the car and were walking north along the sidewalk when we saw a group of people gathered at the center of the Sixth Street intersection. At the same time, we heard a very loud sound, as if someone were breathing very hard. My parents were cautious about joining a group of people like this, but still we rushed to see the excitement. Mom held my hand as we worked our way through the crowd and, suddenly, I looked directly at a man's head lying on its side. He smiled at me and breathed loudly. I was petrified. I looked

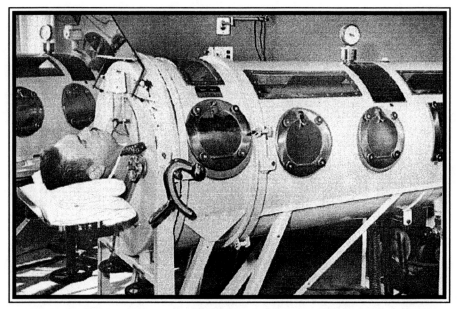

A brave man.

beyond the head to see the neck disappear into a large silver-colored metal tube.

After several seconds, I put things into perspective, realizing that the man lay on his back with only his head free from the enclosure of the machine. With each breath, the machine whirred and vibrated. A nurse assistant stood next to the victim holding an umbrella to protect him from the intense sunlight. A man nearby explained how the "iron lung" worked, and pleaded for the crowd to contribute to the "March of Dimes" effort to help defray costs of providing care for polio victims, and to do research to find a cure. He had us step back and showed us the beginning of a string of dimes placed on the sidewalk next to the scene. Within a few minutes, Dad reached into his pocket for a couple of dimes and placed them end-to-end next to the string. Most of the people in the group rushed with dimes to add to the line. Everyone hoped that we might provide a full mile-long string just from the residents of Emporia.

I shook from this fearful experience while we continued to walk a few blocks farther north and finished our brief shopping. Upon returning to Sixth Street, we walked along the growing line of dimes until we again arrived at the iron lung site. Several men prepared to lift the man in the iron lung onto a flat bed truck and take him back to the hospital. I felt an incredible sympathy for him and tried to imagine how awful that experience would be.

We continued our walk back to the car and saw another strange sight that took my breath away. A carnival had just arrived in town and one of its attractions had been set up on Commercial Street as an advertisement. Walking closer, we saw a crowd assembled in front of a raised platform on the street near the sidewalk. A small booth with a curtain front sat at one end.

A man stepped onto the platform and shouted out that we were about to see the most spectacular sight of our lives. He said that a man from a far-off country had an unusual reaction to drinking water in his town and was slowly turning into stone. The crowd gasped as he walked over to the side of the platform and pulled aside the curtain. There sat a man with a very sad look on his face. As the crowd moved slowly forward, the man's arms, feet and legs came into full view. The speaker encouraged each of us to come close enough to touch the man's arm. It appeared to be solid stone!

Mom and Dad lived in a very real world and it is still hard to imagine that they might be taken in by some kind of trick. However, they were reacting with the same astonishment as most of the crowd. As I stood next to the "stone man," I felt my legs start to fold and cried for Mom to hold on tightly to my hand. I felt incredibly weak and nearly passed out. I do not remember Bonnie's reaction one way or the other. We hurried to the car and Dad quickly drove away.

On the way home, Dad tried to quell our fear of polio and the prospect of living in an iron lung by describing the disease as something which caused a muscle weakness sometimes involving the muscles used for breathing. Perhaps, also, the patient would get better and might soon leave the iron lung. This did work to make me feel better, although he never provided an explanation for the condition of the stone man. Years later, I talked to a doctor who suggested that it might have been an extreme form of ichthyosis caused by a genetic lack of the body's ability to assimilate Vitamin D. Nevertheless, for many years afterward, the sights and sounds of a carnival still made me shaky in my knees!

Chapter 46

"HOW MUCH LONGER before we get to go?" I ask. "Pretty soon—when I get these dishes done," Mom answers. Whew, Mom said "pretty soon," and that's a lot better than "after awhile." I yell at Bonnie to get her shoes on since we are going to leave to the ball game, pretty soon.

On one of our infrequent trips to Olpe, Mom saw a poster tacked to a telephone pole announcing a "Spectacular Baseball Game." Mom stopped the car, got out and ran close enough to the poster to discover that the House of David baseball team would be playing the Emporia Boosters team the following Sunday afternoon. Game time: 2 p.m. at Soden's Grove in Emporia.

Mom later shared her poster discovery with Dad, who immediately started to make plans for the family to attend the game. Dad had discovered this team while working in Chicago several years earlier. He often talked about this "magnificent group of baseball players," each sporting heavy beards and long, flowing hair. He thought attending the game would be a good experience for everyone, including Mom's father, Pop.

The House of David was a national touring team composed of players with talent comparable to many professionals of the day.

Unique with their long hair style, they seemed to be larger than life —
with height and bulk accentuated by their loose fitting uniforms.

Many years later, I discovered that the team originated in a Jewish
community near Benton Harbor, Michigan around 1914. Barnstorming
from coast to coast and in Canada, they soon became popular with
baseball fans across America. They led the way to later baseball inte-
gration, playing such teams as the Kansas City Monarchs of the Negro
Baseball League, whose star was the great Satchel Paige. The House
of David team is credited with playing the very first night baseball
game at Independence, Kansas on April 17, 1930.

The local Boosters team was sponsored by the gas company and
was made up of players living in Emporia. They were considered
more talented than the Stony Ridge Mountain Boys, another area team
which was named after our one-
room school, and which played
its games on the prairie several
miles southwest of Emporia.

My sister and I had never
been to an event in Emporia, so
the excitement built up as the
day approached. Finally the
time came. After church that
morning, we hurried through our
noon dinner and drove the long
15 miles over rough gravel roads
to Emporia. We crossed the
Cottonwood River bridge and
turned right off the road to the
entrance of the Soden's Grove
Baseball Field.

Hairy Giants

A man used a Thomas Lumber Yard nail sack wrapped around his waist to hold change and approached the car and asked for a seventy-five cent entry fee — twenty-five cents for each adult and free for kids. That was unusual to me since ballgames on the prairie were supported by a pass of the hat. As we entered the park grounds, a man directed Dad to drive near a number of parked cars lined up in long rows. This was also a first. Cars parked at Church on Sunday mornings and at Stony Ridge ball games were positioned haphazardly.

We left the car and walked the short distance to the grandstand. At the first sight of the field, Dad let out a whistle, marveling at the magnificent sight of 15 or more bearded giants gliding across the field and hitting batting practice. We slowly climbed the steps at one side of the stadium and found an open section along the bench seats at the end of a row.

I settled in my seat and looked out across the field — the emotion of the moment was intense. I still remember the dark-brown infield and the three white bases so startling in their brightness. Beyond them was the largest expanse of green grass I had ever seen — so much smoother than our pastureland in the spring. Suddenly, I became aware of the crowd gathering around us. This soon became the largest group of people I had ever seen — more than Church on Sundays or movies on the streets of Olpe on hot summer nights. This was also my introduction to the unique sounds of a baseball crowd. An almost constant buzz of subdued voices was accentuated by occasional shrill whistles, jeers and shouts from the fans.

After the players were introduced one-by-one to the crowd, the umpire's shout of "play ball" put everyone at attention. The home team ran onto the field accompanied by a tremendous roar from the crowd. Their white uniforms sparkled in the sunlight as the pitcher threw a few warm-up pitches to the catcher. The House of David team, wearing gray uniforms, managed to hit the ball a few times during that first inning, but I recall no runs being scored.

For some reason, the rest of the game is a blur in my memory. However, I still have the feeling of having belonged to a great crowd. In every direction I looked, I saw activity—men smoking cigars and intensely discussing the game, kids running up and down the stadium steps, and many women visiting. Others fans seemed relaxed and content to simply follow every action on the field. Dad pointed out Joe Brown, a gentleman he knew for many years as a true baseball fan who attended every game in the area. Another fan, Pop Griffith, was positioned directly behind the wire screen about half-way up the stadium seats. He chattered almost constantly and seemed to have an audience close by who followed his every remark. They often chuckled or laughed heartily at his comments. I found out much later that he was the father of my future American Legion Baseball coach and as true a baseball fan as there ever was. I have often wished that I could have recorded his remarks and observations for the pleasure of baseball fans everywhere.

The game ended a few hours later and our trip home was filled with each member of the family sharing observations of an exciting afternoon. I have no memory of which team won, but the team members of the House of David baseball team provided each of us with a happy lifelong memory. I found out years later that the team quit competing during the early 1960s, as other forms of entertainment became more popular.

Chapter 47

Stick Ball

"WHY DON'T YOU and Larry just go over there and ask them if you can play," Mom asks. "They would probably like a few more players," she adds. Larry and I look at each other. They are really big boys, but maybe we should try it.

Cousin Larry was a few years younger than me when my family made the twenty mile trip from our farm to Emporia for our once a month visit with Uncle Chet and Aunt Gladys. They lived in a residential section across the street from the Berg family. Larry and I watched from his back yard while Phil Berg and his friends played a captivating game of stick ball.

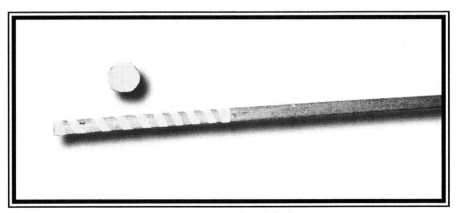

Broomstick and cork ball.

Larry and I were surprised to join the group after we finally gathered the nerve to cross the street and ask if we could play. The field where they played included the Berg's sloping, double-garage driveway and stretched across the street. On our first day, we were selected to the same team to play in the "outfield." That positioned us across the street near Larry's house. We were skilled enough from the playgrounds at our schools to catch a few fly balls and to stop a number of rolling groundballs.

It did not take long to acquaint ourselves with the rules. The stick ball game requires at least two players, but can be played with any larger number. If there were only two players, the batter would toss the ball with one hand and hit it, while still in the air, quickly placing both hands on the bat. If there were three players, they could play as three teams—each player against the other two. If there were four players, there would usually be two against two. The batter would not run the bases since successful hits were mentally recorded. If three players were on one side, there would normally be one pitcher, one infielder and one outfielder.

The post between the two garage doors was the target for the pitcher—and it was also the umpire! If the batter watched a pitch go by and it hit the post, it would be a strike. Of course the high and low pitched balls had to be considered when calling a ball or a strike, but it offered no real argument. Some of the older boys could throw a curve ball far more deadly than a fastball. The ball was sometimes well out of the strike zone, speeding by the batter, before it curved sharply to hit the center post. Anyone who has experimented with throwing a curve with a ping-pong ball knows how difficult it would be to hit.

The ball Phil used was simply a round fishing cork purchased at Hassey's Sport Shop and wrapped tightly with white adhesive tape. The bat was an old, sawed-off broomstick with a taped handle—although Phil once bought an "official" stick ball bat from St. Louis while traveling to watch a Cardinal's baseball game. Baseball fans of today will recognize the advantages of a stick ball bat when they see baseball coaches warm up fielders by using similar looking "fungo" bats. These bats are not legal in official baseball games since they are longer and thinner than regulation bats and provide more control and power. The source of the name, "fungo," has been widely researched but nobody seems to know its origin. An interesting possibility is from the Scottish verb fung, meaning to 'pitch, toss, or fling.'

The foul lines were marked by a couple of small trees on either side of the driveway. All foul balls counted as strikes, and three strikes was an out. Four balls out of the strike zone was a walk—just as in regular baseball. A fly ball caught in the air, or a ground ball picked up before it stopped rolling beyond the near sidewalk, was an out. If the ball reached the "parking" in front of the street, it was a single. A double would be awarded if the ball landed or rolled into the street. A triple would be earned for a hit beyond the street but stopping before the sidewalk across the street. A hit over the sidewalk across the street was a HOME RUN! A monstrous hit would sometimes be stopped by the large trees hanging over the street causing the ball either to fall, to be caught for an out, or score a lesser hit. Many years later, I stepped off the pitcher's distance on the driveway and found it to be about thirty feet and the homerun distance across the street to be a respectable 130 feet.

On rare occasions, brief arguments arose when a ball was stopped by a player when it was directly on a boundary line or when calling balls and strikes. In spite of these conflicts, I recall the game flowing very well and being a pure joy.

One day, Larry and I finally had the opportunity to bat, and what a thrill it was! The light broomstick was easier to swing than a baseball bat, but, since it had a smaller diameter, we had to watch the speeding cork ball much more closely. Once or twice that day, we hit the "sweet spot," and Larry and I both hit homeruns across the street.

I made friends with a number of "stick ball" kids from that neighborhood during this period, including Bob and Dean Morton, Neal Porter, Jesse Gibson, Joe Ryerson, Phil Berg and Jack Taylor, and followed their athletic and professional careers with great interest. From our group, we had a future judge, navy officer, three high school teachers, a local business man, clothing executive, professor and minister. Now, well over sixty years later, many in the group are still active in their professions.

During that first summer, Joe Ryerson took me aside and showed me how to throw a knuckleball. We practiced a number of times. Later, after I injured my arm pitching in college, I resorted to the knuckleball pitch and became somewhat successful in my last varsity year. I often wonder if I had concentrated on that pitch earlier in my career, might I have prevented injury and played baseball at the next level? In any case, on those trips from the farm, I was spellbound by this new game which included so many more playmates than the four students in my tiny one-room school. Perhaps my lifelong love of baseball was born playing stick ball on those beautiful summer afternoons.

Chapter 48

Shooting Stars

"IT'S TOO HOT to sleep anyway, so let's just stay up after dark and try to see a shooting star," Dad suggests. This is going to be so much fun! I better run upstairs and get my blanket to take outside and lie on.

Although Dad read little more than an occasional farm newspaper, like *Capper's Weekly*, he did have a basic appreciation for nature and science. He told us of staying up late at night as a youngster as his older brother Con read by candlelight. Con read every chance he had, but Dad would rest his head on his arm and consider the evening a success if he stayed awake until his brother was ready for bed. Later, during daylight hours working on the farm, Con shared some of his previous night's reading with Dad. This often included science as well as world news and geography.

So, remembering that the best meteor shower of the year usually occurred between August 10th and 20th, Dad chose a very hot night or two to take advantage of the opportunity to spot a "shooting star." My sister and I, along with an occasional cousin or two, would spread our blankets on the concrete house entry. The only view from there would be overhead and directly to the south, because trees blocked our view between the east and west horizons. Dad and Mom would stand farther from the house to get a better view of the full sky and shout out their observations.

It could be either a rewarding or a disappointing experience since a meteor would flash across the sky so quickly that only one or two of the family would see it. I remember that the "winner" observed as many as ten or twelve during the time that we watched—with some of us only seeing one or two. We were constantly reminded that if we could make a wish as we saw the meteor, our wish would come true. I really believed that my wish would come true if only I could say it quickly enough. I recall wanting a baseball bat as my fondest wish. Of course, the meteor would flash by so quickly that it was impossible to "wish upon a star." It was fun, afterwards, to finally get some sleep after straining our necks and forgetting, for a time, the very hot night.

During the days after the meteor shower, Dad loved to relate one of his favorite childhood memories. While living on the Ohm farm a few miles south of Bazaar, Kansas, he saw a meteor appear to hit the ground several yards from the house. He ran quickly to the site and, finding a dirt mound, reached down and sifted the fine dust through his fingers. The dust felt very warm, but it cooled in just a few minutes. He thought the mound was all that was left of the meteorite and that it had completely burned up on landing. But later, after some study, he regretted that he had not dug a few feet under the mound to search for what likely was a solid, and valuable, piece of the meteorite.

In later years, I fondly remembered this experience. It was not until my junior high-school year that Mr. Martin, my science teacher, explained the exact nature of "shooting stars." I eventually had the opportunity to take an "official" astronomy course in college, and became hooked; I taught college astronomy courses throughout my 50-years of teaching.

Chapter 49

"I HELPED DIG several wells when I was a kid on the farm, but one of the most exciting days of my life happened when I was digging that well," Dad said.

Dad started his story by describing in great detail how the digging process progressed. It was easy to dig the first few feet in soft soil. But then Dad and the rest of the crew encountered a heavy sandstone layer requiring picks and sledgehammers to break through. After several more feet, they again met soft dirt, but now time-consuming measures had to be taken to lift dirt to the surface. A rope and pulley system was rigged to pull up buckets of rock and freshly-dug dirt. After the buckets of dirt reached the top, they were hand carried for several yards to spread over nearby pastureland.

When the depth reached six or more feet, the safety of the digger became a concern. Makeshift wood or rope ladders were placed along the well walls for the workers to climb. Finally, after changing shifts of diggers over a period of several days, the water level was reached. Working at this level required knee-high rubber boots when the well floor became muddy. Digging continued for a few more feet to provide a clear space for the water to fill without becoming further contaminated with dirt and mud. Once an adequate depth was reached, it was time to start the very tedious task of laying up rocks around the circumference at the inside base of the well. This was a slow and exhausting job that involved lowering flat rocks by buckets from the surface. The worker below assembled layer after layer of stone until the walls finally reached shoulder height. It then became necessary to use the ladder—slowing the project even more.

Sometime around this point in the dig, veteran diggers encouraged the man at the bottom of the well to look up to the top at the daylit sky. After some uncertainty, most of the diggers located stars against a very dark sky. The farmers of that day declared it a near miracle to see nighttime stars during daylight hours!

When Dad told me this story, he still marveled at the event. In Dad's later years, when I was a physics student, I was able to explain this phenomenon to him. With the dark dirt walls of the well absorbing the scattered blue light of the sky, only light directly overhead survived the depth of the well. Without the bright surrounding sky, light originating from stars directly over the well survived the depth of the well. It is interesting to note that an occasional planet may have been in direct view of the digger, and would have provided a much brighter image as well as a sure cause for excitement.

While a professor in Wyoming, I taught a number of daytime astronomy classes. One of the laboratory experiences asked students to determine the exact location of the planet Venus relative to the Sun. On a given day, the planet might lead the Sun across the sky by a few hours. With its position accurately determined, in a clear, blue sky, the students knew where to try to focus to find the bright, white dot in the daytime sky. Naked-eye sightings were regularly made by most members of the class—much to their delight. Then, with careful direction and a cardboard mailing tube, the planet was seen by everyone in the class. I often think that in using this cardboard tube, I was simulating the sighting by the well-diggers of long ago.

At the conclusion of these laboratory experiences, I often shared my dad's well-digging experience and his ultimate understanding of this amazing phenomenon.

Part Four

Family Memories

*Parents, grandparents,
uncles, aunts and cousins
share by advice and
example useful life
experiences.*

Chapter 50

DAD SAID THAT each of Mom's brothers will attend today's baseball game. That means a bunch of cousins will be there too. I can see the field through the dust. Lots of cars are driving off the main dirt road to the ball field in Al Rathke's pasture.

Although Mom had five brothers, they rarely appeared in one place at the same time. The age difference of eight years gave them different interests and different responsibilities. It seemed that even during special occasions such as weddings and funerals, at least one brother would be missing.

Other than being born and raised on the farm, the brothers had at least four other common interests—horseshoes, pool, poker and baseball. From the early 1920s to the late 40s, at least one of the Schroeder boys could be found on local diamonds playing baseball or fastpitch softball.

Baseball teams were organized to represent numerous one-room schools in the mid-west starting in the early 1870s. Our little one-room school, Stony Ridge, was built in 1878 and within a few years had organized The Stony Ridge Mountain Boys baseball team. The team played into the 1940s against opponents from as far away as Kansas City, Omaha and Oklahoma City. Since transportation was a problem, team members were recruited from nearby farms or small towns. If a family had a number of boys, the team might well be centered around that family.

Walt was the oldest of the brothers, born on the first day of the 20th century: January 1, 1901. He became a baseball standout very early in his life, pitching for the Stony Ridge team at age sixteen. The next brother was Benjamin, (Bud), born in 1904, followed by Frederick (Fritz), born in 1906; then Carl, born in 1908; and finally, Sam, also born on January 1, in 1909. One of the brothers, Earnest, died a few months after birth in 1912.

In addition to baseball, each brother was skilled at playing pool. Pool tables were scarce and no family owned one. Players had to travel to nearby towns with a "pool hall." Saturday afternoons were targeted as a time when some farmers could break away from their daily work routines and compete in games of pool. Pool halls were dark, dingy and smelled of stale beer, but were still found to be an exciting place.

Dad liked to play pool, but rarely did—likely because it cost as much as twenty-five cents a game. In addition to the cost of the games, the men generally drank beer as they played and most matches involved some kind of gambling. As a seven or eight-year-old, I was allowed, on occasion, to visit the pool halls and watch the games in action. I recall seeing dollar bills placed on the side of the pool tables by the players as the prize for winning the game. This competition naturally produced friction that sometimes became volatile—usually not between the brothers but with others from the farm neighborhood. Though they sometimes groused for several days, the brothers calmed down and resumed play during the following weeks.

Dad recognized most of the players in the pool halls, but on occasion he would point out to me a "newcomer" who was perhaps a "pool shark." He said "these guys travel from town to town to try to get local players to play for money." Since they were specialists at playing pool, they many times left with large winnings. I heard stories, though, that some of them met their match and lost money themselves to some of "our regulars."

Some of our happiest times as kids were to anticipate and then travel to Olpe on a Saturday afternoon to sit in our car parked on Main Street. While the men played pool, we watched the people walk by on the sidewalk. After an hour or two, when restlessness set in, Mom took us on a walk up and down the street. I imagine we were then the subjects for observation by other families.

It was rare to see women in a pool hall, unless to retrieve a husband or a son. I remember on one afternoon the door of the pool hall swung open and a lady pulled and tugged on a young man, leading him to a nearby public water well. She held him under the spigot as she pumped cold water over his head. Mom, Bonnie and I were spellbound with the sight as Mom explained that the "kid drank too much beer and his mom was trying to sober him up."

Besides the pool hall gatherings, a special memory of the brothers occurred during a very hot evening during the summer of 1946. Carl's fastpitch softball team was to play a make-up game that evening but, with short notice, several team members phoned to say they could not play.

We had just moved to town into a house with a full basement. Having no air-conditioning, the basement was much cooler than the rest of the house and Carl and Dad decided to have an emergency meeting there to try to organize a team before the 9 p.m. starting time. My sister and I watched Dad and Carl begin planning the quest for a full team. Dad ran upstairs a number of times to make phone calls to prospects including all of Carl's brothers. As the early evening progressed, brothers Fritz, Bud and Sam all showed up in our basement.

The only other time I recall as many as four brothers in one place was occasionally at the poker table.

The seriousness of their mission to field a full team dominated the scene. Facing a forfeit just an hour before game time, Dad called one of the most feared pitchers in the county, Laverne Miltz . He accepted the invitation to pitch but asked for a five-dollar fee. The brothers agreed and donated a dollar each. Dad agreed to play as well, but "right field only." He did not feel confident in his playing ability and hoped that this assignment would require less talent than any other position on the field.

Bonnie and I were very disappointed since the polio scare did not allow us to follow the men to Peter Pan Park in Emporia to watch the game. We stayed up until Dad got home and he shared his very exciting account of winning the game against one of the best teams in the league.

Though they shared a passion for sports, the vocational destinies of the brothers varied from "Fritz, the super salesman," to "Bud and Sam, the oil-field workers," to "Carl, the roofer." Walt, the oldest, ultimately bought the family farm and spent his working life there. Fritz was the only brother who saw military service in the Army in Alaska.

Many years later, I was a baseball pitcher for Emporia State University. As I took my warm-ups before game time, I noticed that the umpire behind the plate was my Uncle Fritz. I waved to him and he nodded his head in recognition. During the first inning, I walked four batters and hit two others—giving up seven runs before being removed from the game. While on the mound it seemed that each and every pitch I threw resulted in Uncle Fritz waving his left hand for a called ball. Struggling with the worst pitching performance of my career, I wondered if the umpire remembered that I was his nephew. Likely, though, having to call my awful pitching, he felt as badly as I did!

Uncles: Fritz, Walt, Sam, Carl and Bud

Stonyridge Baseball Team
1916

Uncle Walt makes the team at age 15.

Back row: Bud Rice, Walt Schroeder, George Funk, Joe Rathke.

Sitting: Bill Rathke, Happy Jack-Alfred Verona, Herman Mockry, George Dieker, Albert Gramke.

Chapter 51

Chicago and the Mob

"I REMEMBER THAT John Dillinger, Pretty Boy Floyd, and Bonnie and Clyde were all killed by the FBI when I was working in Chicago," Dad says. *I've heard these stories before, but Dad likes to tell them and they sure are exciting.*

Dad had lived and worked on his family's farm for most of his first twenty-six years. After completing high school, he enrolled for one year in a business college in Wichita, but was called back home because of the illness and death of his mother. The next two years were quite turbulent as his father re-married, merging two families including several children. After his father became ill and died, Dad found farm work in the area. Restlessness soon took over and during the fall of 1933, he decided to accept a work offer from an uncle in Chicago.

He packed his guitar, a few changes of clothes, and his dog, Laddy, into his Model A Ford. Upon arrival, he was assigned as a delivery man for his uncle's specialty sausage company. The job turned out to be very demanding because it required long hours and heavy lifting, all the while sleeping in an attic above the sausage factory.

Chicago bound.

Dad traveled throughout the city and observed happenings that astounded and troubled him. His customer deliveries included bars, speakeasies, restaurants and other establishments with no easy definition.

City newspapers sensationalized the daily activities of the considerable criminal element. Dad soon learned the names and characters of various mob groups and their members and followed their activities both in Chicago and in other parts of the country. On some of his deliveries, workers shared their experiences while watching the likes of Al Capone, George "Machine Gun" Kelly, "Pretty Boy Floyd," Bonnie and Clyde, John Dillinger and many others. They told stories of visitations to their business establishments, and of the mobsters' companions, dress and manners. Several of these "gangsters" were killed during Dad's stay in Chicago and the resulting press coverage served to crystallize the events in his mind.

After about a year, Dad decided big city life was not for him so he returned to the Bazaar, Kansas area and once again began to farm. Soon after, he met my mother and they were married on March 1, 1935. He threw himself into the obligations of raising a family and, with the beginning of World War II, soon worked harder than he had ever worked before—first on an oil lease near Winfield, Kansas, and then on Mom's family farm.

It took very little encouragement to get him to talk about his Gangster Era experiences. He was able to describe in some detail many of the crimes of the key figures, invariably ending with the way they died. It is likely that many isolated farm families of that day lived a little "dangerously" while following the exploits of these famous outlaws. Perhaps it is not unlike the public's fascination with crime stories in today's movies and television.

I knew that I had been named after the western movie star, Ken Maynard, and asked both Mom and Dad if my sister Bonnie was named after the famous gangster, Bonnie Parker. I recall that they looked at each other momentarily before denying it. Years later, I asked my ninety-year old mother once again and she replied, "No, we would never have done that." But Bonnie and I still wonder.

Chapter 52

Crash Landing

"LET'S PLAY THE airplane crash game." Cousins Larry, Herman, Lloyd, and Edgar have just piled out of their cars for a visit to Pop's place this Sunday afternoon. "Varoom, varoom, putt, putt, putt! Here comes the airplane over the hill. Its motor is sputtering and it is losing altitude," Larry shouts. We all start pretending we are airplanes with our arms extended straight out as we whirl around and run in large circles.

The story of an airplane's emergency landing on a late fall afternoon in 1930 has been enthusiastically relayed to generations of Schroeders. Uncle Walt and Aunt Martha lived on an 80-acre farm just north of Pop's farm. Walt worked in the corral near the barn when he first heard a distant sound. He noticed something very unusual about the sound of the approaching airplane. Unlike an engine's normal smooth drone, this one sputtered intermittently.

Walt spotted the plane in the eastern sky as it descended quite rapidly toward him. Seconds later, he recognized the plane's profile as it prepared to land on a smooth section of pasture, a short distance to the south. The engine was barely running when the wheels touched down. It plowed through the high grass and skidded sideways to a stop.

Uncle Walt ran, vaulted a couple of fences and sprinted up to the silent airplane. The door opened and a woman stepped out. "Could this possibly be the famous Amelia Earhart?" he thought. He imagined that this was the famed woman pilot and his farm might become the center of national attention by the following day. When a man followed the woman out of the small airplane door, Walt introduced himself and asked them if they were all right. The woman greeted him with a "Yes, but we have some serious mechanical problems and will need to use a telephone as soon as possible." She said to Walt, later, that when she exited the plane a few minutes earlier, the cattle in the area approached her. She thought that the bright red jacket she was wearing caused the cattle to charge her, so she quickly reentered her airplane, took off her jacket, and waited for help.

Walt did not catch their names as he led them back to his house. Chickens, dogs and other animals announced the visitors with loud, cacophonous sounds. Martha came out to greet them and, as was the custom in all rural areas at that time, inquired if they were hungry. They said that they would love to share something after they made a telephone call. Left alone on the porch as the call was made, Walt and Martha excitedly exchanged concerns about what to have for supper and when. Should they invite the visitors to stay overnight and, if so, where would they sleep? Should the bed sheets be washed yet this evening? What should they serve for breakfast the next morning?

They decided that the new arrivals would sleep in Walt and Martha's bedroom, while Walt and Martha would sleep in the kids' room. The kids—all three of them—would sleep on the porch as they often did on a hot summer night.

After they called authorities in St. Louis, the two pilots agreed to stay overnight. They said that officials would arrive tomorrow to decide what to do with the airplane. Walt and the visitors then walked back across the pasture to the landing site. On the way to the plane, Walt learned that the woman pilot was Marjorie Doid, a well-known woman aviator, but definitely not Amelia Earhart. Furthermore, the airplane was a sister ship of the famous *The Spirit of St. Louis*, and was on its way from the west coast to take part in a number of air races near Cleveland, Ohio.

Meanwhile, Martha excitedly telephoned everyone on the party line to relate the story of the "crash landing." She asked them not to come over since the pilot might be Amelia Earhart and she should not be disturbed as her airplane was being repaired. Martha even boasted that she had called the *Emporia Gazette* and that they were going to send a reporter to the farm in the morning.

After some time, Walt and the guests walked back to the house where Martha was informed that the woman was not Amelia Earhart and the man was only her mechanic. Since the visitors were not married, it was decided that the woman could have the main bedroom, and the gentleman, the kids' room. Walt and Martha would have to share the porch with the youngsters.

Everyone visited for several hours after supper and retired for the night. Early next morning, Walt stepped out of the house to begin chores, leaving Martha to prepare breakfast. He was greeted by several carloads of people waiting to view the stranded airplane. Although he quickly dispelled the rumor that Amelia Earhart had landed, the crowd still wanted to see the airplane. Walt ignored his chores for a few hours and led them to the plane—firmly asking that they not walk too close to it.

By ten o'clock in the morning, the visiting couple had traveled in Walt's car to Olpe to shop at Diebolts General Department Store. Marjorie Doid wore the pilots' cap of the day, a leather jacket, neatly pressed trousers and shiny boots. She was overheard several times during the visit describing with surprising obscenity her dislike for this airplane engine with its inability to fly when "pouring on the coals."

Two men with a large flatbed truck arrived about noon. They quickly checked the airplane and, after opening a cylinder and finding metallic pieces, decided that it could not be repaired in the field. They needed to load it on the truck and transport it back to St. Louis. By then, dozens of visitors were available to help with the disassembly and loading. Late in the afternoon as the loaded truck prepared to leave, the guests insisted on giving some money to Walt and Martha and their kids for their hospitality. A few days later, Sonny, Gilbert, and Geraldine arrived at Sunday school with new clothes purchased with the money from those wonderful people who arrived out of the sky!

Chapter 53

"DAD, DO YOU think we will find anything today? We have walked over this ground lots of times and haven't found anything, yet." "Maybe today we will find an old blasting cap or a piece of a wooden box. It is kinda fun to look around," Dad says.

South of our little 80-acre farm, two streams flowed side by side, some 200 yards apart. They bound a level area that holds a well-known place of sadness to this day. This same area was the site of an emergency airplane landing just a few years earlier in 1930.

During that winter, Panhandle Eastern Pipeline Company laid one of their 28-inch pipelines directly across this area. Their main camp was on the flat site between the two streams. A large quantity of dynamite was necessary to blast through the rock to help dig a wide trench through these Flint Hills of Kansas. Cases of dynamite were stacked along the edge of one of the streams, and the stack acted as a windbreak for the campsite.

On this particular day, a man connected blasting caps to the dynamite sticks that were to be used later. He lit a small fire nearby to help keep warm. He apparently left the windbreak for a short time and the fire spread into the dry, surrounding grass. The man ran back trying to put out the fire, but was too late. The fire reached the cases of dynamite and the whole stack exploded!

A neighbor was feeding cattle in his pasture about a half-mile away. At the time he heard the explosion, he turned around to see the smoke and debris that rose an estimated 300 feet. My uncle Walt, who owned the farm where the pipe was laid, was much closer to the site and the blast's shock wave knocked him off his hay wagon, gave him a concussion and he temporarily lost consciousness.

Several farmers from the area soon extinguished the resulting fire. After searching the area for a number of days following the tragedy, all that was ever found of the employee was a piece of jawbone!

Just a few days later, in the section just north of the dynamic blast, there was another tragedy. A huge trenching machine was struggling to remove blasted rock from the pipeline ditch. With its 30-inch wide tracks straddling the ditch, a worker jumped in to dislodge some of the rocks. As he attempted to jump back out, one of the tracks crushed him. The loud noise from the engine prevented the operator from hearing his screams although a fellow worker, some 100 feet away, saw the accident and ran to help. The man was dead before the machine could be stopped and backed away.

Over the years, as the story was retold by neighbors who saw it, one could see the sadness in their eyes. Although they did not know either one of these men, they had great sympathy for fellow workers who tried so hard to earn a living during these desperate times.

Chapter 54

A True Cowboy Hero

"MOM, TELL US about the fire on the roof." It is a cold, dark day and Bonnie and I have nothing to do until chores. We have heard the story many times, but it always gets Mom excited to talk about it and it sure is fun for us kids. Mom starts, "I was coming in from the chicken house..."

Just a year before Mom was married, at the age of 17, she had been feeding the chickens in the yard near the house when she looked up at the roof over the living room and saw white smoke. She ran into the house yelling to her younger sister to get outside. She then telephoned the central operator in Olpe. "We have a fire at the Schroeder house," she screamed.

Joe Cooper had come in early for lunch after working cattle. He lived about three-quarters of a mile to the northwest of the Schroeder house. Since lunch was to be a quick meal, and he expected to go back out to the pasture, he had left his horse saddled. As soon as he sat down at the kitchen table, the emergency telephone ring sounded. He answered and found that a fire had been reported from his neighbors to the south.

Without hesitating, he ran out, jumped on the horse and raced to the house. He jumped several fences along the way and arrived in minutes. As he arrived at the house and saw the smoke, he steadied his horse and jumped from the saddle to the roof. He tore the smoldering shingles from the roof with his gloved hands. By then Mom had finally alerted her brother Carl. He and Pop rushed in with water buckets dipped full from a rainwater barrel. These, along with soaked gunnysacks, were handed up to Joe. He doused the fire in several minutes. Close inspection showed a break in the metal chimney lining that had allowed flames to ignite the surrounding shingles.

Before leaving for home, Joe stayed around for several more hours to help repair the damaged roof. The Schroeder family expressed gratitude to him with an offer of homemade bread and fresh pork chops. There was no doubt that without his immediate reaction their home would not be standing as it is now, some 125 years after it was built.

I recently followed the possible path of this famous ride and found at least four fences and two ravines still existing between Joe's home site and that of the Schroeder place. It is easy to envision that adventuresome ride some 75 years ago.

Within days, word had spread throughout the county about this dashing cowboy who had leaped his horse over high fences and wide

Lonely Spurs

ditches to fight the fire. As years went by, I not only heard the story repeated by my mother, but also by Dad. Many uncles and aunts offered their version as well. In public, Cooper always wore cowboy boots with his pants legs tucked inside and a large white cowboy hat. While attending social events in town or in our one-room schoolhouse, people would often point and whisper, "See that handsome man over there. That's Joe Cooper who saved the Schroeder house."

Joe mysteriously moved away several years later. Some thought he would head to either Texas or Mexico. Although friends and family tried to make contact, none was successful. Eventually, a report reached some of the family that the unidentified skeletal remains of a man about 50 years old were found on a lonely, wind-blown prairie in Texas. Furthermore, a bullet hole was found in the skull. No weapon was found near the scene. Conjecture was that the victim had been a cowboy and was likely to have been in an argument and shot. Another possibility was that he was thrown from his horse and, while severely injured, used a gun on himself. The gun may then have been found and stolen. If it were Joe, it was a sad ending for a true cowboy hero.

Chapter 55

Another One-Room School

MY COLLEAGUE AND friend, Lyle Baker, asks if we should stop and take a picture of Atyeo School. "No," I reply. "We better keep driving as we need to get to the Cassoday Café before it closes at three." We pass by the old schoolhouse and it looks very lonely. We can see the stump of an old tree to the west of the building.

One-room schoolhouses across the mid-western farmland were normally constructed about 5 miles apart—or at a distance that re-quired no more than a 2 ½ to 3 mile walk for the students. This was considered a reasonable walking distance for first-grade children as young as six years old.

We knew that our school, Stony Ridge, had neighboring schools, but we never visited them. In some parts of the country, however, regular competitions in debate, music and sometimes athletic events were held between students of one-room schools. I believe that in our situation there were logistical and financial problems. Roads were very poor, especially during the winter, and vehicles and gasoline were at a premium. Also, the nearest one-room school to ours was almost ten miles away! It was built at a time when no farm homes existed in the large pasture land area to the west and, therefore, had no school-age children requiring a near-by school.

Atyeo School was situated on a gentle hill near the main gravel road extending about eight miles along the same road passing by our farm. It had a reputation as a well-kept, well-attended facility. The teacher, Elizabeth Kinsey, was recognized as an excellent teacher and was admired by both students and parents. Perhaps the unique characteristic of the school was the existence of a single, mature tree a few yards to the west of the schoolhouse.

The kids in the school used this tree for welcome shade during lunch and recess time in the spring and fall. One of its large limbs supported a chain swing. In addition, climbing the tree was a favorite sport—although not encouraged by Miss Kinsey. As part of the last-day-of-school activities, however, all students in the school, along with the teacher, were allowed to climb the tree for a group picture.

The only contact between students of our two schools was in our Lutheran Sunday School. Distances between churches of a given denomination were much farther than those of one-room schools. This resulted in some interaction with kids from other schools, but the strict discipline of Sunday school classes and church services allowed little visiting time. We did find out, however, that recess games were quite similar. "Annie-over," hide-and-seek, crack-the-whip, fox and geese during snow season, and, of course some form of baseball were played by all. But, for Atyeo, the most noteworthy discussion point was the magnificent tree "right in the front yard!"

After three years teaching, Elizabeth retired, married one of my oldest cousins, Gilbert, and moved to the family farm. A long life followed, raising five children, and supporting a fully active farming and cattle operation. Gilbert passed away in 2002, but Elizabeth still lives on the home place.

My friend Lyle and I recently took our annual drive past my home farm and the site of both Stony Ridge and the Atyeo School. Regretfully, the buildings have been removed and only the foundations and the Atyeo tree stump survive to stimulate fond memories. We missed our chance for future generations to have an image of the Atyeo School, but at least one photo of the Stony Ridge pupils from 1937 remains to help bridge the gap to the future.

Stony Ridge School — 1936-1937
Front row: Louise Schmidt, Geraldine Schroeder and Ruth Hinrichs. Second row: Clara Mockry, Allene Jones (hidden) and Florence Rathke. Third row: Wayne Schroeder, Gilbert Schroeder, Bob Rathke, Elmer Mockry, Lee Rathke and Lawrence Gramke. Fourth row: Walter Schroeder, Helen Rathke, Jim Rathke, Raymond Hinrichs, Warren Rathke and Robert Rathke.

Chapter 56

Spit Shine

EDGAR AND I can see our faces in Gilbert's shoes! How does he get his shoes so shiny? "It's called spit shine, and we do it every day in the navy," Gilbert replies. "If we find some shoe polish, will you help us do that to our shoes?" Edgar asks.

Buying and maintaining shoes was a big part of household concerns during World War II. Rationing became a way of life. Careful study and budgeting preceded each purchase, whether for adults or for kids. I remember a number of times when part of an evening was spent counting change on the kitchen table in anticipation of a shoe purchase. Because shoe prices ran into the high two-dollar range, which was a major part of the weekly budget, we had to save up and account for every penny.

We generally planned a shoe buying trip in a nearby town during August. This became part of the "shopping for school" experience. The smell of genuine leather wafted through our nostrils, as we entered the shoe store. The wide variety of shoes available today was not available in those days. We had little concern for style, but ruggedness and lasting quality was a must. This resulted in high-top "clodhoppers" as the only choice for me. The salesman brought out a few different sizes with color choices of black or brown. My parents preferred brown. I tried on a black pair, but deferred to their better judgment. The shoe size was fitted to "grow into," so they would flop around, at first. Yet, by the time we grew into them, the shoes had worn out.

We were never allowed to wear the new shoes out of the store. We had to wait until we got home to carefully put them on and wear them in the house. Close inspection of the sharp, ridged design of the soles made us feel that they could "make us run faster." They needed "breaking in." After wearing them in the house for several days, we could finally wear them to Sunday school and church. Once outside, we could not resist trying to run up the side of a tree or a large rock to check out this "new found" foot power. They even made it easier to climb trees! But, after several weeks of "Sunday only" wearing, and after an occasional muddy accident, we were finally given permission to wear them to school. We wore the last year's shoes sparingly in the rocky, more dangerous fields and on Sundays during the barefoot summer months.

I remember wearing my new shoes for the first time several weeks after school started in September. The old, tight, holey shoes were always good enough to last "a few more days." To extend their use, we often placed a small piece of heavy cardboard inside the shoe to cover holes in the sole. This was a last ditch effort to extend the shoes' life.

People told us that shoes came from cow hides just like we had on our farm. This was a little disarming! We did not want to associate our cows' destiny with the materials making up our shoes.

In the fall of 1944, my cousin Gilbert was on leave from the navy. He was home to marry Elizabeth—beginning a fifty-five year relationship. My family was living on "Pop's" farm at the time, and it was the center of wedding-day activities. Gib showed up in his white dress uniform, with the shiniest black shoes we had ever seen. The many younger cousins were awed by his appearance and pleaded with him to show us how to polish our shoes like his. I ran to Mom and begged her to let us use the ten-cent tin of brown Shinola shoe polish stored in the pantry.

With a few rags and our shoes in hand, Gilbert carefully instructed us for several minutes. He showed us how to apply the polish to the toe of the shoe, spit on it, and rub very hard and fast with a clean rag. For some of the older kids, a nice shine suddenly appeared, while for others, we could never see a difference. We worked hard for the next hour or so, spitting on our shoes and buffing them as hard as we could. We finally decided that to get a perfect shine, we needed black shoes and had to be very powerful—just like Gib.

In my later years, as a physics professor, I discovered a number of factors that help to achieve a mirror-like shoe shine. Although the sailors and soldiers used saliva for their shoes shines, water works just as well. Since shoe wax does not mix with water, the spit acts to keep the buffing rag from absorbing too much polish. Saliva also applies pressure to the polish—rather than the rougher rag. This pressure forces the coat of polish to be very smooth and thin, therefore, shinier.

Shiny shoes.

But, as Gib pointed out, a spit shine could never appear after just one shine... or two shines... or three. Maybe it took thirty or forty spit shines to make shoes look as good as his. And, regardless of how many hash marks for length of service a sailor displayed on his blues, or how many campaign medals he had earned, nothing revealed his military attitude better than spit-shined shoes.

Little did we know at that time that Gib's pride in his spit-shined shoes exemplified one's lifetime goal—to be at his or her best at all times.

Chapter 57

Blue and Yellow

"I THINK I see a little blue," Mom says. Bonnie and I only see white. Dad says we need to wait a few weeks before we decide if it works or not.

A significant part of a farm house-wife's duties was weekly clothes washing. The mechanics of the washing itself were considerable, but adding chemicals to make white clothes brighter and starching before ironing were almost separate sciences and quite time consuming.

After using either a washboard or a powered washing machine, a small amount of liquid chemical bluing was added to a tub of clear water as a final rinse for white clothes. During my days on the farm, bluing offset the natural yellowing of white clothes.

Mom's insistence on white extended to her white kitchen cabinets. With two wood burning stoves in our house, the cabinets yellowed soon after being painted and required a new coat almost yearly. After considerable deliberation, Dad figured that if bluing worked for clothes, it might also work with white paint on our kitchen cabinets.

I clearly remember the day Dad brought home a pint of blue paint and a gallon of white. He wanted to try his experiment, although Mom was visibly concerned that her cabinets would turn blue. Dad reconsidered mixing a full pint of blue paint to the white and decided to try only a half-pint. After several minutes of stirring with a wooden stick, Dad asked each of us to look at the mix. Mom, likely biased, said she saw some blue, but Bonnie, Dad and I saw pure white.

With some hesitation, Dad began painting and, after the job was completed, invited visiting friends and relatives to give their opinion of the finished product. Everyone claimed that these were the whitest cabinets they had every seen! For the next several months, Mom critically eyed her white cabinets. She finally admitted that the experiment was a success. Even after several more years, no major yellowing was observed. Perhaps the blue paint mix had been tried by someone else, but my dad concluded this to be his true and original scientific discovery.

A few years later, I rediscovered bluing in Mr. Martin's seventh-grade science class. He demonstrated how mixing yellow and blue light produced white light. He also described how a few drops of bluing, mixed into a final water hair-rinse, turned gray hair into a beautiful white. As another example, he explained that the popular white side-wall automobile tires of that day were sold with a blue, water-soluble covering. An initial washing then exposed a brilliant white side-wall. He then set up a salt-crystal or "Coal Garden" experiment to grow an impressive and colorful crystal display.

To duplicate this experiment, several chunks of coal or charcoal may be placed in a throw away pie tin. Mix one-fourth cup of water, one-fourth cup of bluing, one-fourth cup of non-iodized salt with a tablespoon of ammonia and pour over the coal. Then drip several colors of food coloring on separate locations over the coal. After two days, pour a solution of two tablespoons of water and two tablespoons of ammonia around the edge of the coal. Watch the magic!

During the school experience of each of my four children, I suggested they build a coal garden for one of their science projects. It was such a delight to be reminded of those days on the farm and to Dad's great enthusiasm for "discovering" a means for making cabinets "whiter than white!"

Mrs. Stewart's magic.

Chapter 58

"HERE COMES POP," Bonnie shouts from the back seat. Mom opens the window and waves at him. With a big smile, Pop walks over and, pulling the cigar stub from his mouth, rests his crossed arms on the car door, leans over and begins to visit with us. The car fills with the familiar aroma of cigar smoke.

All of my uncles on my mother's side of the family either smoked or chewed tobacco, sometimes both. Popular in the thirties and forties, a wad of tobacco bulging from one cheek or the other, or a protruding, chewed cigar was a facial characteristic of many farmers. Nearly all farmers and many of their wives were regular cigarette smokers, as well. In today's terms, it might be considered an epidemic. In nearly every movie of the day, including our favorite westerns, as well as in magazines and newspapers, tobacco use was glorified as a treat for everyone. Tobacco use was an enthusiastic subject of table and casual conversation across farm country.

Most often, tobacco was purchased in cloth sacks or pouches from grocery stores or pool halls. Thin, white paper sheets were carefully rolled around a line of tobacco to produce cigarettes. The hand-rolled versions sold for much less than the ready-made cigarettes purchased in packs. A smoker shelled out extra money for a factory cigarette only on special occasions.

Another special treat was rolling cigarettes and using a much fresher tobacco purchased in a sealed can. These small, colorful cans were found in the kitchens of most contemporary farms. Their tall, thin shape did not work as an ashtray, so regular coffee, vegetable, or small syrup cans were used instead. Most of my uncles had their own ash-tray can. They just tossed them outside when they were filled and found a new one. The original tobacco cans were better-used, however, to hold nuts, bolts and other small items on the workbench. It is interesting to find these tins on the shelves of antique stores today with asking prices of several dollars.

Kids of that day naturally imitated smoking behavior. It seems that grown ups disapproved of very early use of tobacco by youngsters. However, by the time kids reached twelve years old, many had tried smoking and chewing tobacco. Many stories related the incredible nausea associated with the first "chew." Some youngsters swore off tobacco forever after a severe reaction. As a means of imitating a cigarette, corn silk or crushed, dry grapevine leaves were collected and rolled into a piece of paper from a newspaper or from catalog pages. The dried stem of the grapevine itself was sometimes used. If a kid could manage to find a match, a smoking "cigarette" was then produced. The resulting bitter, acrid, harsh smoke deterred many kids from trying the "real thing."

I remember that Dad lectured me about how smoking resulted in acquiring a very severe habit. He did not seem to object to the activity as it related to health, but he held that a smoker would be captured for life with an habitual need that would always be present. He also made the unusual request—one that most parents made of their children—that if I started to smoke, to please not hide it from him. I did not question that request until many years later. How could that possibly be important to him? Would Dad have thought of me as being hypocritical if I tried to hide my smoking from him?

Since the idea that smoking might be harmful to one's health was rarely considered, dangers from second-hand smoke were not considered at all. I recall traveling by car to church or to town on a winter day with the windows tightly closed. The air inside was blue-white with smoke. When traveling with friends and other relatives, the same condition surrounded us. My reactions to these pollutants explain my lifetime of asthma and bronchial attacks.

My strong resistance to smoking was likely due to my associated illnesses. But as a young junior high student, my coach and gym teacher, Mr. Bell, got my attention with a stern lecture. He said I would never be a good athlete if I smoked. To this day, I remember that exact place and time, and I so appreciate his effort.

Prince Albert in a can.

As difficult as it was, at age seventy-one, and after sixty years of smoking, Dad quit "cold-turkey." Although he lived another five years, they were made difficult because of smoking-induced emphysema. He had to have oxygen supplied to him using a face mask, and his movement was limited to just a few feet. Among the last words he spoke to me was a plea to share his plight with my children, grandchildren and as many others as possible about the dangers of smoking. I took his request seriously and believe that his experience has deterred a number of kids from following this dangerous path.

Chapter 59

DAD IS SITTING on a big rock outside. As I run toward him, he yells at me to "Stay clear--don't get close to this knife!" I sit close enough to see the beautiful, milky-white curls following the blade as it cuts across the block of wood Dad holds in his left hand.

Whether it just relieved stress or gave him a chance to fill a few idle minutes, Dad's attention to whittling was not predictable. His search for the perfect piece of wood, however, showed good judgment. When we cleared brush and trees on our farm land, or when we visited neighbors, Dad carefully inspected sections of the tree branches and searched for small blocks of cut wood in nearby woodpiles. When he found a sample with grain and texture conducive to smooth and even carving, he stored it on a shelf in the tool shed. "Some of the tree limbs need to dry a bit," he said.

The pocket knife he used had two blades of different sizes, and he kept them sharp. Along with the knife, Dad frequently carried a small sharpening stone about the size of a pack of gum. With the knife blade fully sharpened, he produced an extra-sharp whittling edge by stropping the blade on his leather belt.

Dad experimented with all kinds of whittling subjects, but windmills and birds were his specialty. He started each project in the same

way. After choosing a piece of wood, he "eye-balled" the major di-
mensions for the envisioned product, and scratched several lines along
its length. He placed the knife blade at one end of the wood piece,
and slowly pulled the blade through layer after layer. It was a spectacular sight to watch a bird's feathers become distinct one by one,
first on one side of the wood block, and then the other. If one looked
closely, the layered "feathers" showed a small separation from each
other. Depending on the composition of the wood block, the grain
might show a unique and startling pattern of varying colors.

I remember Dad whittling flying birds with outstretched wings
and fanned tails, but other times creating roosting birds with wings
tightly clamped around the body and tail feathers that formed a tight
band stretching behind the bird. The bird's head was created next,
as Dad carefully manipulated the tiny knife blade around one end of
the block.

The only time I recall Dad seeming to daydream was while he
whittled. In today's terms, he would appear to be in a meditation or

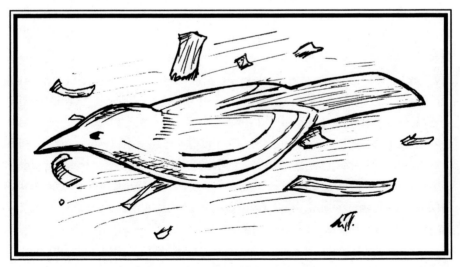

A Miracle out of wood.

trance-like state. Otherwise, he was quite intense in his daily life. Mom, however, often enjoyed sitting quietly during special moments "staring into space." She continued this habit well into her 90s.

Once the bird's head and beak were completed, Dad focused attention on forming a smooth, round breast with just a hint of tightly bound feathers. The final touch before completion was to darken the bird's eyes with a lead pencil. I remember after he finished one wooden bird, a tiny, dark knot formed the exact position of an eye. Whether he planned this or not, Dad never said. No paint was used on these creations, although Dad frequently talked of "finding paint to finish the job right."

Sometimes, after a few minutes of whittling on a new block of wood, the blades of a windmill might take form. This created a special excitement for my sister and me because we could enjoy playing with a moving toy.

The circular windmill, with six or eight blades, was completed when Dad bored a hole through the center of the array by spinning the blade of his small knife. This reminded me of the technique used to relieve blood pressure from under our fingernails after an injury. Each member of our family, at one time or another, had a small hole drilled with a knife point into a smashed fingernail.

With the windmill-carving completed, a small nail was driven through the hole into a long stick or thin tree branch. This provided a handle for Bonnie or me to hold as we ran across the yard, causing the windmill to spin. Finally, after we kids were exhausted from the running and excitement, Dad would place the windmill into the ground to spin in the wind. Although quite beautiful to see, the fragile windmill soon became disabled. Even though Dad had taken many hours over several days to finish the project, he did not seem discouraged. For some reason, Dad showed little interest in these projects after completion, but he frequently started another one soon afterwards.

On rare occasions Dad whittled various flower designs and invented other subjects such as vertical branches or rods featuring broad, lengthy curls along the full height. He stored many unfinished pieces on shelves in the barn or workshop, but they, as well as all completed pieces, eventually disappeared. Like so many other broken things in life, I would give a lot to hold even one of Dad's whittling projects.

Chapter 60

Two Ringers and a Leaner

"WE WILL HAVE one pit under this tree, and the other one over there in the sun. You can start digging right here," Dad said. We are going to have our own horseshoe pit. This is going to be fun!

Once in a great while, Dad came home from the oilfields some-what later than his usual time. He arranged with Mom to hold sup-per so that he could play a few games of horseshoes with his fellow workers. These contests took place near a new drilling site or next to an established oil well, making it easier for the workers to gather.

Crowding the stake.

Dad always arrived home with a story for the whole family. He boasted about how many games he won, then bragged about his total number of ringers. Regardless of the won-lost record, the players took great pride in winning the ringer count. Dad shared these results with enthusiasm, declaring that he would start practicing more and take the game much more seriously. After considerable sacrifice, Dad saved enough money—about four dollars—to buy an official set of four matching horseshoes. He planned to carry them in the company truck each day and practice during lunchtime and after work. This never came to pass, however, as work and family duties generally dominated his time until another match might be scheduled.

Two metal stakes, each surrounded by a soft dirt pit, made up the horseshoe pitching site. The pit allowed the horseshoes to "stick" where they hit instead of rolling some distance away. If the workers found a little extra time during the day, or at lunch time, they would dig two four-foot squares in the dirt, some forty feet apart, to soften up the soil. If sand were available, they mixed it with the dirt to form a soft landing place for the horseshoes. Acquiring stakes should have been easy in an oil field, but it was a struggle—sometimes resulting in the use of flimsy, hollow metal pipes. Ideally, solid metal rods, about three or four-foot long were driven into the dirt at the center of each square for the target. We had no standard rod sizes as shafts from worn out farm machinery were commonly used. Both rods leaned about three inches toward the opposite pit to better grab the horseshoe after a direct hit.

Dad loved to talk with me about horseshoe pitching technique. An older oil-field co-worker had qualified for the Kansas state championships in the early 1930s. He had shared his knowledge with Dad and became a hero in Dad's eyes.

When I became old enough to pitch a horseshoe a few feet, Dad demonstrated how to hold on and pitch it. His two favorite grips resulted in the shoe either turning 1 ¼ or 1 ¾ times in its flight, before landing at the stake for a ringer. With the horseshoe held at arms length in front with the opening up, and gripped at the lower right curve, a horizontal delivery resulted in a 1 ¾ turn for a ringer. For a 1 ¼ turn, the shoe opening would be down and gripped on the side. Since each throw required a different height and a certain adjustment for wind conditions, the chosen grip had to be practiced time and again before reaching the required consistency.

Dad's release was incredibly smooth, and the horseshoe would sail with a slight wobble to its target. His delivery was unique, however, in that he led with his right leg. Most right-handed athletes lead with their left leg when throwing or tossing things. Dad's technique required moving his hips to the left to allow more room for the arm swing. This produced a rather strange over-all body motion and I could recognize him from some distance, even when he was pitching with several other players. Dad claimed that he could tell at the instant of release whether or not he would score a ringer. In fact, he would often let out a happy yell as the horseshoe was in flight to the stake. I fondly recall when he would throw 10 or 12 ringers in a row. During several matches, he threw nearly 70% ringers against oil-field competitors who cancelled about 75% of Dad's successes with ringers of their own. I remember him practicing throwing ringers at target stakes that held one or two horseshoes leaning against the stake. The "leaner" scored two points versus the three-point ringer, but offered a considerable obstacle for the next thrower. Dad suggested that each throw was too valuable to waste on knocking away the opponents' horseshoes, so he practiced pitching ringers between the leaner and the stake. During one practice session, I clearly remember Dad pitching two consecutive ringers directly under a leaner!

In Dad's later life, when I was an adult, we would occasionally pitch horseshoes—using his original, "official" shoes. I could not get the proper spin however much I practiced and when the shoe hit the ground, it often rolled several feet away. Finally, I resorted to gripping the horseshoe at the base causing it to flip several times on the way to the target. It seemed like an effective way for me to throw a ringer—but not nearly as effective as Dad's horizontal spin method.

Eventually, Dad's health failed and he quit throwing horseshoes. He presented me with his original set of horseshoes in his hand-made, wooden toolbox. I still have the shoes in the toolbox stored on a shelf in my garage. Perhaps tomorrow I will go out and try that 1 ¼ spin—maybe leading with my right leg!

Epilogue

MY FRIEND, JOHN, and I stand at the crest of a hill overlooking the entrance to the Bazaar cemetery about a mile away. "I can give you some private time with your family if you want to visit their gravesites," John says. "No, my folks are with me each day, wherever I am," I reply. "We might trim the rose bushes surrounding my granddad's headstone, though."

After living at one edge of the Flint Hills on my mom's family farm during the early years of my life, my deep connection with and affection for the hills continued to evolve over a life time.

My first teaching job in Manhattan, Kansas allowed me to continue my exploration of the Flint Hills. I joined the Kansas State University Flying Club in 1960, giving me the opportunity to view the uniqueness of the Flint Hills in a wide range of conditions. Daytime trips over the landscape gave meaning to the phrase, "sea of grass," often used to describe the area. Depending on the season, the waving grass may give way to a more barren, rock-coated view. Hunks of gray-white limestone, sometimes called "mutton rocks" by geologists, appear almost in formation on the slopes of the hills.

The most striking air view comes in early April when the prairie is intentionally burned by ranchers. Most of the pastureland is alternately burned in two or three year cycles, providing a contrasting air view from year to year. These burning cycles, along with cattle grazing on tall bluestem grass, and a dynamic climate, sustain the hearty ecosystem. The rocky soil and steep hillsides limit growing crops, except in river and creek bottoms.

Although daytime burning provides stimulating views, when flying over the region at night, the fires present an unparalleled panorama. Against a pitch-black background, gentle wafts of white smoke lift from the meandering yellow bands of fire. Soon after the burn, grasses and prairie flowers erupt on the blackened surface. Within days, even when flying high over the hills, the view from horizon to horizon is dominated by green interrupted by slashes of streams and bordering trees.

Upon returning to Kansas after living and teaching in Wyoming for over twenty-six years, I made countless trips to my mom's family farm, some forty miles east of my dad's home place, and visited many other small communities within the Flint Hills.

Just twenty miles to the north of my dad's family home farm, sits the Tallgrass Prairie National Preserve, the only grassland park in the United States. Whether in the Park, or on the pasture lands in the region, walking the hills reveals varying signs of flint and limestone.

These rocks were deposited during the Permian Period of geologic history, some 280 million years ago, when a shallow ocean covered this region with a tropical climate. Remains of marine life on the floor of the ocean became limestone—imbedded with chert (flint). Clay and mud were deposited as well and were compressed to become shale. The ocean floor became the surface of the modern Flint Hills and, since the floor was of the same age and composition, weathering was uniform. Softer shale regions became valleys while the limestone and flint capped the hilltops. A significant characteristic of the hilltops, then, is their common height; they are, to a large degree, the same altitude. Standing on a hilltop and turning in a circle presents a straight-line horizon in the full 360 degrees. It gives the observer a unique sensation of standing on top of the world and a wonderful feeling of belonging to the earth!

In the low country along the creek bottoms, corns, soybeans and other cash crops help support farmers in the area. This region is criss-crossed by gravel roads maintained by large, yellow road graders. Over the years, I had a number of relatives spend their working years grading and caring for these critical passageways. Those with whom I visited showed an incredible sense of duty—even when working through the night after heavy blizzards or rains. Snow drifts, often several feet deep, were plowed from the roads and, many times, from the lanes leading to the farmhouses. Rains occasionally swept away parts of the roads producing repair needs that required hand work as well as heavy machines.

While traveling the gravel roads, encounters with the residents in-variably result in a greeting by a lifted finger or two from the steering wheel. The courteous reply is an in-kind signal. Many miles of lime-stone fences can be seen along stretches of these roads. Government subsidies were paid to farmers to construct much of this rock fencing beginning in the late 1860s. Most of them were laid by hand, stone by stone. They offered a sufficient barrier to contain livestock and to establish boundaries. Tax breaks were also given for every one hundred feet of planted Osage Orange trees. We called these trees, "hedge," and planted them along section lines as a windbreak and as an aid to help hold livestock. Today, many hedge rows still stand proudly.

Scraping out a living from eighty acres in the Flint Hills has been a task that occupied three generations of my family. Dad was born and raised near the little town of Bazaar, in the heart of the Flint Hills. Called Franz by his family and later Frank by my mom's family, he spent his early adulthood laboring on his family's farm. With only brief interruptions, he lived his seventy-six years either in the Flint Hills or in their shadow.

At times, when he was able to separate his painful memories of long-ago hours of hard labor in sub-zero winters and in scorching summers, he shared a genuine love for the Flint Hills. When given an interested audience, he fondly told stories of his early days which included details of his daily activities. Many of his stories are included in my books, but others sometimes flash anew in my mind after being lost for decades.

Although none of his brothers or sisters is buried in the Bazaar Cemetery, Dad decided early-on to make his eternal rest with his parents. After several years of on-again, off-again deliberation, he finally purchased a four-site plot on the side of a gentle slope in the cemetery. The asking price was twenty dollars.

At the same time that Dad purchased his headstone, Mom agreed that she would be buried there as well and that a headstone should be purchased for her. This would be the "efficient way to deal with such things." That is my conviction as well.

The Flint Hills is a special place. It is a region of little traffic, crime, resentment, or trouble. It is more a place of friendship, trust and happiness—a nice place to find peace and a nice place to retire.

And so, dear Flint Hills, the day is nearing when I will join my family just a few feet below your historical ground surrounded by your unending peace and serenity. My memories of your hills and valleys, towns and people, are the signature of the Supreme Architect of the universe—whose promise of eternity is validated by his guidance of Ducks Across the Moon.

Dad's home farm — 100 years later.

Mom's home farm — 100 years later.

Also by Dr. Ken Ohm

Spatzies and Brass BBs: Life in a One-Room Country School

In this autobiographical memoir of farm and school life in Kansas during the early 1940s, Ohm describes his grade school years in one-room rural schools. The first school, Sunnyside School, was located north of Winfield, Kansas, and the second, Stony Ridge School, was southwest of Emporia, Kansas. Stepping back in time, the reader will experience accounts such as "Clodhoppers and Overalls," "The Pot-Bellied Stove," "The Pump Handle," "Meadowlarks and Sunflowers," "Tornado Alley," and "Christmas on our Very Own Farm." Anecdotes, illustrations, and photographs deliver the simple beauty of life in rural Midwestern America.

ISBN 1-58597-278-9 (soft cover edition)
ISBN 1-58597-289-4 (hard cover edition)

ABOUT THE AUTHOR

After the success of his first book, *Spatzies and Brass BBs*, relating to his early experiences in one-room rural schools, Dr. Ken Ohm now provides a personal glimpse into the daily lives and times of WWII-era rural Kansas. He spent his early elementary school years with his family as they scraped out a living on an eighty acre farm in the Flint Hills. His lifelong fascination with the Hills is reflected in unique details of this special place.

The author earned his bachelor's and master's degrees from Emporia State University in Kansas and his doctorate from the University of Wyoming. Nearing the end of a fifty-year science and mathematics teaching career, he currently teaches mathematics at Washburn University in Topeka, Kansas. After winning two recent national senior championships in the javelin throw, he attributed his success to throwing flintstones at fence posts during his early childhood days in the Flint Hills.